D0820378

The Center for South and Southeast Asia Studies of the University of California is the coordinating center for research, teaching programs, and special projects relating to the South and Southeast Asia areas on the nine campuses of the University. The Center is the largest such research and teaching organization in the United States, with more than 150 related faculty representing all disciplines within the social sciences, languages, and humanities.

The Center publishes a Monograph series, an Occasional Papers series, and sponsors a series of books published by the University of California Press. Manuscripts for these publications have been selected with the highest standards of academic excellence, with emphasis on those studies and literary works that are pioneers in their fields, and that provide fresh insights into the life and culture of the great civilizations of South and Southeast Asia.

RECENT PUBLICATIONS OF THE
CENTER FOR SOUTH AND SOUTHEAST ASIA STUDIES

FRANK F. CONLON
The Saraswat Brahmans in the Modern World

EDWARD CONZE
The Large Sutra on Perfect Wisdom

GEORGE L. HART, III
The Poems of Ancient Tamil:
Their Milieu and Their Sanskrit Counterparts

ROBERT LINGAT
The Classical Law of India
(translated by J. Duncan M. Derrett)

M. N. SRINIVAS
The Remembered Village

The Transport of Love

This volume is sponsored by the
CENTER FOR SOUTH AND SOUTHEAST ASIA STUDIES,
University of California, Berkeley

Bharut Stūpa. Pillar relief.
Early 1st century B. C.

The Transport of Love

The <u>Meghadūta</u> of Kālidāsa

Translation and Introduction
by Leonard Nathan

University of California Press
Berkeley . Los Angeles . London

For My Students

University of California Press
Berkeley and Los Angeles, California

University of California Press, Ltd.
London, England

ISBN 0-520-03031-1
Library of Congress Catalog Card Number: 75-13157

Printed in the United States of America
Designed by Geri Davis

Contents

A Note on Sanskrit Pronunciation and Naming   vii

Introduction   1

A Note on Texts   14

Meghadūta   15–89

Appendix I: Commentary   91

Appendix II: Finding List   111

A Note on Sanskrit Pronunciation and Naming

The problem of preserving accurate Sanskrit pronunciation in English is, strictly speaking, insoluble. Certain sounds in the former have no equivalents in the latter, a fact which makes Sanskrit names often sit uneasily in English texts. But total Anglicizing rings false to my ear, whereas preserving the original as faithfully as possible seems mere professorial fussiness. I have taken the middle way. Thus, in my translation, Sanskrit ś and ṣ conflate to English *sh*, while the vowel ṛ becomes *ri*, a trill concluding with the faint hint of an *i* sound. In other ways I have followed convention, so that retroflexion is noted by a dot below the letter, and the long *a*, *i*, and *u* are represented as ā, ī, and ū. These, with the other long Sanskrit vowels (e, ai, o, and au) should be given double the duration of the short vowels. In *Kubera*, for example, the second syllable is lengthened, sounding most like the *a* in "shape."[1] Pronunciation of Sanskrit vowels should approximate "Italian values."

[1] The reader of English must resist the temptation to put stress either where it would fall in our language, Kúbera, or where the original calls for length, Kubéra. Sanskrit poetry observes vowel length and pitch, but if accent is present in it at all, it is not heard enough to count as a significant metric effect.

When a flower or tree in the original had a common English equivalent, I have tended to use the English. On occasion I have translated a Sanskrit name into its literal significance when I thought doing so would be more informative and would spare the need for a note. Thus, for *Pushkarāvartakas* (stanza 6), I give "The Whirlpools," the family name of a race of clouds. Sanskrit proper nouns tend to be metonymic epithets, but I have let these stand where they seemed familiar enough to Western readers who would recognize Shiva but not "Auspicious One." Sometimes, however, I have converted a less well-known epithet to a more familiar one—a liberty taken, again, to avoid notes. But the damage in any case seems minimal because usually the epithet that Kālidāsa chose was more a matter of metrical than semantic urgency. Such substitutions are in fact more justified in Sanskrit than in most other languages, since Sanskrit is deliberately artificial, its ties with vernaculars having been decisively severed early in the development of the literature. Its words thus do not have as great a connotative resonance as those of "natural" languages, and the Sanskrit poet is thus relatively freer to choose from among the vast bank of its synonyms for the word that will fit his sound pattern. Unlike Western poets, he is not constrained to weigh the difference in nuance among several words that signify almost the same thing. Any word meaning, say, "king," will do. This semantic interchangeability is part of the genius of the language, affording the poets another tool for their art.

So Sanskrit poets never put real toads in their imaginary gardens. This fact provides a little consolation for the translator of Sanskrit verse, who sometimes can feel that he is merely engaged in setting the untranslatably exotic in the too elegantly native. And he can also hope for the good will of the reader who has some notion of what is involved in this worthwhile if unaccommodating enterprise.[2]

[2] The reader is also invited to note the detailed commentary in Appendix I, which can be used either as an aid for interpreting the poem or simply as a glossary of Sanskrit names as they appear in the reading. The Finding List of Appendix II briefly defines these names for quick reference.

In the final analysis even the idea that the great deeds and the beauty of the world require song to praise them is founded on the knowledge that the individual thing is limited, imperfect, in need of completion, and that even greatness perishes, while song is indestructible, and beauty depends on the "wise" for its manifestation. And evidently it is up to the wise man to show that the world discloses its greatest beauty in the wealth of its correlations, through its correspondences and contrasts: nay, that the essence of this beauty resides in the agreement and balance of its parts.

BRUNO SNELL, *The Discovery of the Mind*

"Give me the news of my dear one, Oh cloud!"

Introduction

*From oriole to crow, note the decline
In music. Crow is realist. But, then,
Oriole, also, may be realist.*

WALLACE STEVENS

The *Meghadūta*, or *Cloud Messenger*, like most classical Indian poems of any length, is an affirmation of its author's culture. It is more indirectly so than Kālidāsa's two longer poems. One, the *Raghuvaṃsha*, celebrates the royal line of which the great hero Rāma was part; the other, *Kumārasambhava*, treats the birth of the war god, Skanda, Shiva's son, and his victory over the demon, Tāraka, whose power threatened the divine order of things. Whereas these two poems openly exalt the values of a culture, the *Meghadūta* does so only obliquely, but with no less intensity. For, what looks on the surface to be a charming invention having little to do with the great issues of human governance and universal order, is in fact an elegant tribute to the idealized Indian landscape in which those momentous concerns found their native soil.[1]

[1] It is a bit dismaying to see no less an authority than S. K. De praise the poem's "splendid natural scenery which enchances its poignant appeal." (*Megha-Dūta of Kālidāsa* [New Delhi, 1957], p. xxxii.) Underlying this praise is a realistic criterion of literary value wholly alien to the poet of the *Meghadūta*. Its application here only breeds confusion. However, in fairness to Professor De, this remark is followed by a far more perspicuous one: "In the earlier part of the poem the description of external nature is heightened throughout by an intimate association

1

The *Meghadūta*'s entire "action" is embodied in the long apostrophe of an exiled minor deity, or Yaksha, who asks that a cloud carry his message of devotion to his far-off mate. In this apostrophe, the Yaksha describes for the cloud its appropriate northward itinerary, and in so doing maps out a country permeated with the lore and legend that summon up many of the deepest values of Indian life.

Places are imbued with meaning because they have been the setting for memorable deeds or events or because they provided home or refuge for great personages. Moreover, through a transformation of the Yaksha's anguished desire, geography, flora, fauna, and even cities become humanized participants in one of the most poignant and persistent motifs of Indian culture—love in separation, which in this instance goads the lover's imagination to dwell on love in union. So mountains and rivers are invested with feeling and their beauty charged with sexual attraction; trees and flowers become their ornaments. Animals evoke human beauties: for example, the timid eyes of a deer call to mind glances of shy girls. Even time is made an active agent here, for the poem opens at the beginning of the rainy season—hence the presence of a cloud—that moment in India which traditionally marks the joyous reunion of lovers parted by distance or circumstance; even the great rains act out the release of pent-up passions.

It is as if the culture demanded of its poets that nothing be left out, nothing be regarded as inanimate, nothing be treated as alien to the human; the results are like a great ceremony in which each step affirms the value of the life humanized by participation.

But this ceremonial quality is precisely what is most apt to put off a modern Western reader, for it seems to leave out the very things we value in the art we regard as authentic. Where we look for close adherence to psychological and physical reality, the Indian poet rigorously excludes verisimilitude. Where we

with human feeling, while the picture of the lover's sorrowing heart in the later part is skillfully framed in the surrounding beauty of nature." (*Ibid.*, pp. xxxii-xxxiii.)

expect the poet to speak in his own voice—a voice that should be at once close to common speech and yet identifiably original— the Indian poet stays far behind his subject and strives at every turn for uncommon eloquence which yet deliberately echoes the voices of his tradition. Where we are prepared for, if not direct conflict, at least strong tension needing drastic resolution, the Indian poet gives us the slow unfolding of a foregone conclusion.[2] Where we might hope to feel the pleasure of new insight, the Indian poet wants his audience to experience the delight of a foreknown universal sentiment. In short, the poet was not expected to bring raw news of himself or the world, to lay out the complexities of social relations, or to flash light on the dark interior life of the particularized soul. He was asked instead to proffer the experience of the ideal, all the flaws of nature corrected, all the unfinished aims of men completed, everything in its proper place, performing its proper function in an orderly, therefore beautiful way. Kālidāsa, in short, could not have imagined an audience composed of readers like us.

Behind Indian poetic expectation and the poems addressed to it were two major assumptions that we do not share. First, that reality was not to be sought through personal sensory apprehension of our changing empirical world, but beyond it to one that is permanent and ideal. One way the latter could be apprehended was through language that matches the ideal in its permanence and perfection. That language was Sanskrit in its poetic mode. Poems, then, were a way of experiencing the reality beyond appearance, and the pleasure one derived from reading or hearing them was, in the view of respected critics, analogous to the personal bliss arrived at by the religious experience of the divine truth. The second assumption concerned the hierarchical social system developed in India from Vedic times. This system was, according to the traditional view, based upon the

Plato

[2] Eric Auerbach's distinction of foreground and background styles is of some use here. The Sanskrit poets, like Homer, employed the former insofar as they seem to exhaust their subjects and bring events forward "in leisurely fashion and with very little of suspense." (*Mimesis*, trans. W. R. Trask [Princeton, 1953], p. 11) But the parallel does not entirely hold and should not be pushed too far.

3

rock of divine order. To understand it was, therefore, to approve it, realizing its faults to be the result merely of the shortcomings in those who failed to adhere to its rules, to *dharma*. The unspoken contract between Kālidāsa and his audience assimilated these assumptions so thoroughly that they enter into every element of the *Meghadūta* and must be kept continually in mind if we are to understand what its proper audience experienced in the presence of the poem.

But that understanding is not easy to come by, since it is not primarily a matter of intellectual conviction, but of something deeply grounded in the Indian feeling for life and culture. The West, while it has had its idealist tradition, has largely treated the phenomenal world as a real one, no matter what lay beyond it. And while we have had our own poetry of affirmation, we have a powerful and highly valued tradition of adversary literature, in which the established order is by no means regarded as reflecting a divine or ideal one. Homer, hardly a rebel, obliquely called into question the heroic society of *The Iliad* in which honor was measured by the quantity of booty a man could boast of.[3] But from the nineteenth century on, our literature has more and more been an adversary one, until, today, a Western poet who praised the state would be regarded as something like a traitor to his art by fellow poets and much of his public.

How then is a contemporary American reader able to put himself in the place of the Indian for whom Kālidāsa composed? Perhaps the best way is to attempt to reconstruct the process of an actual reading itself. How might it have been for a cultured Indian to turn to the opening lines of the *Meghadūta*, that critical moment in which the poet establishes his stance toward both subject and audience? Transcribed into the Roman alphabet, the Sanskrit looks like this:

> kaścitkāntāvirahagurunā svādhikārapramattaḥ
> śāpenāstamgamitamahimā varśabhogyena bhartuḥ/
> yakṣaścakre janakatanayāsnānapunyodakeṣu
> snigdhacchāyātaruṣu vasatiṃ rāmagiryāśrameṣu//

[3] See E. M. W. Tillyard, *Poetry Direct and Oblique* (London, 1948), pp. 42–43.

4

One of the first things to notice without benefit of translation is the lack of internal punctuation, except for the break between lines, which, however, signals a pause in meter only, not in sense.[4] This absence is significant if it is recalled that Sanskrit poetry is recited, not dramatically, but in the manner of a chant, its meter (measured by syllable length and number) conducing to a highly musical quality.[5] Another plainly visible characteristic of the passage is word length, some of which is only apparent, where separate words are joined for euphony, as with the first cluster in which *kaścit* is really a single unit. The remainder, however, constitutes a compound of a very Germanic sort making a single unit. Typical of Sanskrit verse, this coalescing of words, added to the absence of stops and the strong flowing cadence, induces a great forward fluency of sound. And this fluency is enriched by other sound patterns: complex vowel echoes, for example, and elaborate repetition of consonants. Thus the movement of the stanza, which is usually taken as a separate unit of syntax and meaning, is one of considerable momentum,

[4] There are , in fact, other pauses within the line, these between metrical feet, but such pauses are characteristically not related to the unfolding of meaning.

[5] The meter of the *Meghadūta* is the *mandākrāntā*, a fixed pattern of short and long syllables that critics have found especially suited to the subject of the poem, as other patterns are suited to other subjects. The assumption here is that there is a correspondence between the quality of certain subjects and the auditory effect of certain meters. We find a like claim in Western criticism, where the iambic meter presumably sorts well with heroic or solemn topics, as the trochaic with lighter ones. There is an important difference to be noted, however: our iambic has been traditionally exploited as a dramatic device to control or modulate tone. That is, the metrical pattern is established as a tonal norm so that variations from it, along with shifts in sense, produce differences in the "voice" of the poem. The model for such usage (always excluding more songlike meters) is, in fact, spoken language. But the model for Sanskrit usage is the chant, and, therefore, meter functions not to change or modulate tone, but as a richly complex (and thus never boring) medium for sense. The fact that there are different styles of reciting the same meter only argues against any indivisible articulation of sound and significance. Nor do possible tonal changes accompanying changes in tempo or volume of reciting suggest any more than that sound "echoes" sense; for these changes would be adumbrated by the over-riding cadence of the chanted meter and any tonal modulation derived from them would be, at best, of a very general sort.

given fullness by the accumulation of patterned resonance. And when it is remembered that Kālidāsa composed with recitation in mind, the importance of the sound of the poem cannot be underestimated.[6]

But this tonal momentum has no parallel in the actual flow of sense. In fact, quite the reverse, as a word-by-word translation into English reveals. In the following, even if only the Roman script of each section is read first, and then the italics, the meaning is arrived at with considerable labor:

1. A certain *on account of lover-separation-heavy* having failed in his duty *curse* deprived of his glory *to be endured for a year of his lord*,
2. Yaksha made *in the Janaka's-daughter-ablution-purified-watered thick-shade-treed* (his) dwelling *Rāma-mountain hermitages*.[7]

Of course the original, based on different syntactical expectations, is not quite so difficult. Still, its sense is by no means easily assimilated. For example, the subject-predicate (Yaksha ... made ... dwelling) is all but lost in a maze of modifiers. Because Sanskrit is a highly inflected language, the poet is free to place words pretty much where he wishes in a sentence and still count on world-ending and context finally to clarify grammatical relations. But I use the word "finally" advisedly, because as the first stanza unfolds, it cannot be clear to auditors or readers how the sentence will turn out. *Kaścit* ([a] "certain") does not pick up what it modifies, *yakṣa*, until the second half of the stanza; in the meantime, a considerable amount of modifying material, unattached to its noun, has been offered, and the audience must suspend its judgment through long compounds, themselves requiring some analysis, until the noun is brought forward. Even then the sentence is not resolved, for the object of the verb must wait through more compounding until the penultimate word

[6] The tradition of oral presentation is still strong in India, despite the impact of the printing press. In Kālidāsa's day, recitation probably would have been the primary means of "publishing" a poem, especially in the milieu of the court, which was where Kālidāsa would have looked for his proper audience.

[7] This means of showing the order of the original as directly as possible I owe to a suggestion of Professor D. H. H. Ingalls.

of the stanza. Then, as with a jigsaw puzzle when the parts are all set in place, the sense is completed.

It is clear that the experience of hearing or reading such a composition must involve tension between the strong and easy flow of its sound and the obscuring hesitation of its significance. But this tension, far from indicating a fault, is one of the exciting possibilities available to the Sanskrit poet. For he can play these oppositions off against each other as a composer plays one melody off against another, deepening interest by controlled complication.

This complication is an essential and characteristic effect, yet not the whole. For *what* the words are saying must also be closely observed. In the first stanza, for example, the Yaksha is introduced by the use of compound modifiers, which act rather like epithets describing his state of affairs. We learn from these that he has been banished a year for some failure in duty to his lord (Kubera, the god of Wealth). Immediately, the choice of a Yaksha as the apparent subject would itself be significant to an Indian audience. These minor deities could be viewed in Kālidāsa's time as rather neutral figures, more often benign than not.[8] That Kālidāsa has not selected for this role, as he might have, a well-known character from legend, and that the Yaksha is not even designated by a proper name, would signify that he is probably not the poem's primary subject. Too vivid a character would have interposed between audience and landscape, the actual subject of the poem. The one positive trait of the Yaksha, aside from his very human desire, is his supernatural status, a sort of credential for his ability to describe nature as seen from the clouds and for his acquaintance with the marvels of the divine city of Alakā, which serves as a sort of geographical climax to the poem. Indeed, if there is any real character in the *Meghadūta*, it is the cloud, who, through the Yaksha's erotic imaginings, becomes a sort of magnetic center for the complex associations

---

[8] Though in earlier literature, Yakshas could be terrifying demons, Kālidāsa's Yaksha is merely a manlike being with supernatural powers; since his master has deprived him of these powers, he is for all practical purposes human.

of all things in the world. But this development is built slowly in the later stanzas.

The Yaksha's character or very lack of it, then, directs audience expectation to some degree. But the locale he has chosen for his exile, as described in the opening lines, does so more intensely. For Rāmagiri (Rāma's Mountain) is the site of another and far greater exile, with this crucial difference—Rāma was banished *with* his mate. Yet the pathetic contrast here is only heightened by the knowledge that Rāma's wife was abducted during their exile. This separation is one of the most melancholy in Sanskrit literature and one which every reader or auditor of Kālidāsa would have had by heart. So the motif of love in separation is announced immediately, and powerfully re-enforced by invoking the parallel of Rāma's exile. The emotions associated with that motif will permeate the rest of the poem and, as I noted earlier, invest the landscape with an intensely human significance. Indeed, in his description of Rāmagiri, Kālidāsa has already begun to transform the landscape into more than something beautiful to behold. Rāma's one-time presence has sanctified the mountain, given it significance as part of the great moral saga of the overthrow of evil by god in human form. Some of its sanctity even preceded Rāma's coming, since it had served as a refuge for holy men. Further, its waters have been purified by the chaste Sītā's bathing in them. Since mountains and waters will be two major features of the landscape treated in much of the rest of the poem, the hallowed locale of the first stanza signals the series to come.[9] All, like it, will be transformed into active agents in a love poem, but not love in the sense only of the passion of creature for creature, but also of the spirit for its home, the Indian poet for his world, idealized and celebrated by the converting powers of devotion. Nor does it matter whether natural objects are used to ornament human beauty or the human used

---

[9] The allusion to Rāma and Sītā is echoed in stanza 97, close to the end of the poem, where Sītā's eager attention to Rāma's messenger while she is a captive of the demon king is used as a comparison for the attentiveness the cloud messenger will receive when he reaches the Yaksha's mate.

to express the beauty of nature; it is all one thing in the ideal world, whose beauties are interchangeable or related through a profound correspondence of great to small, high to low, supernatural to natural.

By the end of the first stanza, Kālidāsa's audience is set well on the way that the poet has chosen for it. Surprised it may be from time to time by his invention or craft, but never disappointed. The opening counterpoint of flow and sense sustain the rich unfolding of the Yaksha's intense longing, which in turn works its transformations on the landscape.

Indian critics have tried to set forth the nature and purpose of classical poems and to a great degree have succeeded, though to our modern way of thinking their dicta may seem overly dogmatic. Thus, Daṇḍin prescribes what is to be included in the *mahākāvya*, a long poem composed in high style and compassing a variety of ornately amplified topics:

> descriptions of towns, oceans, mountains, seasons, the rising and setting of the sun and moon, sports in parks or [by] the sea, drinking, lovefeasts, separations, marriages, the production of a son, meeting of councils, embassies, campaigns, battles, and the triumph of the hero though his rivals' merits may be exalted.[10]

If this appears to limit a poet's range of invention, it must be remembered that the Sanskrit author cared little for novelty; it was not his aim to keep his audience attentive by giving it new information but rather by richly exploiting old subjects. And though the *Meghadūta* is regarded as a *khaṇḍakāvya*, a shorter poem also in high style but compassing fewer topics, it includes, if only by suggestion, some of the items Daṇḍin mentions as essential. That it does so is hardly an accident, for Daṇḍin's catalogue is no arbitrary selection of things that he thought might be helpful to include in poems. It constitutes, rather, an accurate guide to the traditional topics that had engaged the imagination of poets whose purpose, it should be remembered,

[10] A. B. Keith, *A History of Sanskrit Literature* (London, 1961), p. 92.

was to celebrate their culture. The favored topics in all instances are wonders of a sort, that is, matters susceptible to the rhetoric of praise.[11]

If the poet's general purpose with respect to such topics was to glorify them, his purpose with respect to his audience, according to some of the most authoritative critics, was to create a blissful state, liberated from the impurities of personal involvement. Thus, even fear and horror could be enjoyed, again through transformation, this time of basic emotions into a purified senti-ment, say, of grief into compassion, so that the spectacle of life could be contemplated as viewed by a deity from above. It is a brilliant stroke of Kālidāsa's to portray his country from far above, as seen through divine eyes. Such vision puts all in its proper place and gives its witness the aesthetic pleasure of the wholeness that makes all its parts significant. Moreover, from this lofty view the landscape takes on the beauty of idealized distance. Sanskrit poets seemed to work best at this distance, a fact which may explain their lack of interest in realism and autobiographical revelation.

This latter lack of interest helps in itself to explain why we know so little about Kālidāsa, not enough even to place him in time with any certainty.[12] Whereas modern poets often date each version of a manuscript, Sanskrit poets seemed content to let their actual lives be assimilated to legend, becoming in the process ideal types of the poet.[13]

[11] Bruno Snell remarks that Virgil in his *Eclogues* "does not narrate facts or events at all; he is more interested in the unfolding and praising of situations." (*The Discovery of the Mind* [New York, 1960], p. 291). This might equally well be said of Sanskrit poets in much of their work. And the same impulse—to praise—may help explain the fondness of Sanskrit poets for hyperbole, one of the strongest devices for glorifying, just as the fondness for the pun may be explained by their sense of the correspondence of things.

[12] One view that receives considerable support is that he was a court poet of Chandragupta II (A.D. 375–414) at Ujjayinī. See, for example, L. Renou, *Indian Literature* (New York, 1964), p. 21.

[13] Sanskrit critics did not neglect this matter either. The character and training of the ideal poet were set forth in some detail. See *La Kāvyamīmāmsā de Rājaśekhara*, trans., N. Stchoupak and L. Renou (Paris, 1946).

Kālidāsa has been generally recognized as the best example of the ideal, perhaps because so little is known of him, but mostly because he is acknowledged to be the greatest of Sanskrit poets. He composed the three poems already mentioned, and possibly another, the *Ritusaṃhāra*, (*The Round of Seasons*). But he is best known for his *Shakuntalā*, a play that has had considerable popularity in the West. Two other plays are ascribed to him: *Vikramorvashī*, and with less certainty, *Malavikāgnimitra*, neither as impressive as *Shakuntalā*, though, like it, dominated by the sentiment of love. Other works are ascribed to Kālidāsa because his name is like a magnet and because the general indifference to chronology and to the preservation of autobiographical data makes it possible to affix titles to names with the faintest plausibility.

In the works generally recognized as his, there is a special mark, an unpedantic eloquence (unusual in its relative simplicity compared to the work of most other Sanskrit poets), a fullness and sweetness that give a sense of beautiful completion. Goethe tried to convey this in his hyperbolic praise of *Shakuntalā*; for him that very name summoned up both new blossom and ripened fruit, earth and heaven, what wholly satisfied and delighted the soul, that is, what communicated a marvelous sense of things fulfilled from beginning to end and the joy of that fulfillment at every point. And though critics have not found Kālidāsa faultless, his work surely is a remarkable example of Indian classical culture in its highest achievement.

If the modern American reader wishes to experience something of that achievement, he must hold in abeyance some of his own preconceptions; but, also, he must come to the original through translation, which, as someone has said, is the wrong side of the rug. At best it may contain intimations of the original greatness. It also is at best a narrowing, more or less drastic, of the scope of the original. I have, in an effort to make the narrowing less drastic, tried to keep a flowing cadence (though the music of the original is beyond translation) and also, as far as English allows, the counterpointing complexity of syntax, a choice which has made my version more Yeats than Williams or Pound. In an

11

earlier version I tried the mode associated with the latter two poets and which dominates contemporary poetic convention in America. But it seemed to me that to break the flow into clots of intense image, much as Christopher Logue has done with Homer, was to seek a false modernity at the expense of Kālidāsa's intention. To put it another way: using the imagist or free style would have gotten a far smaller percentage of the original than the more traditional mode I have chosen, no matter how fashionable Kālidāsa could have been made to appear. It would be like refashioning *Paradise Lost* into *Paterson* or *The Cantos*. The results might be brilliant but not Milton. So I have deliberately risked the charge of being obsolete in the hope that the reader would be willing to meet me halfway or at least remain open to the possibilities of a convention that seems just now to belong to the past. I should add, however, that I have kept the diction of my version as modern as possible. No "thys" or "thous," no archaisms. Kālidāsa's language is elevated (all Sanskrit kāvya aims at high style) but not out of the range of his proper audience. I have said that he is no pedant. Besides, as Robert Goldman has remarked in another connection: since Sanskrit is an immortal language, the only tongue that serves for its translation is the one that seems immortal to us, our own.

I wish here to thank Professor Goldman for that wisdom as well as for his sound advice on many other points concerning this project, and to include in my deep gratitude those who have given me of their time and understanding in this project: Kenneth Bryant, John Gage, Daniel Melia, Josephine Miles, Vinayak Paranajpe, Thomas Sloane, and Barend Van Nooten. I also owe Professor D. H. H. Ingalls of Harvard a considerable debt of thanks. Denis Lahey, James Ebin, Sally Sutherland, and especially Keith Jefferds have all worked with me under the title of assistant, but were more like collaborators and, more often than it is comfortable to admit, teachers. In Miranda Ewell I found that ideal combination—a typist who is both impeccable and unruffled by an author's hairbrained last-second changes of mind. My wife exerted her great sensitivity and patience in helping me prepare

12

the text; and an old friend, Margaret Rebhan, tempered my vast generalizations on things Indian by her sobering questions.

I wish here to express my gratitude for the University of California Creative Arts Fellowship that made available the leisure to complete this work.

It is usual to say at this point that the faults herein are the author's and his alone. I wish that I could find some way to dodge this commonplace. But alas, truth is truth.

A Note on Texts

I have based my translation mainly on the text found in S. K. De's *The Megha-Dūta of Kālidāsa* (New Delhi, 1957), particularly with reference to the authenticity of stanzas and their ordering. I have referred extensively also to the edition of M. R. Kale (Bombay, n.d.), and that of E. Hultzch (London, 1911), less so to *The Cloud Messenger*, the well-known translation by Franklin and Eleanor Edgerton (Ann Arbor, 1964). I have from time to time consulted a number of other texts and translations: V. S. Nerurkar's edition (Bombay, 1948), G. H. Rooke's version (London, 1935), that of R. H. Assier de Pompignan (Paris, 1938), that of H. H. Wilson (Varanasi, reprinted 1961), and the text of the edition of N. B. Godbole and K. P. Paraba (Bombay, 1890).

Meghadūta

कश्चित्कान्ताविरहगुरुणा स्वाधिकारात्प्रमत्तः
शापेनास्तंगमितमहिमा वर्षभोग्येण भर्तुः ।
यक्षश्चक्रे जनकतनयास्नानपुण्योदकेषु
स्निग्धच्छायातरुषु वसति रामगिर्याश्रमेषु ॥ १ ॥

तस्मिन्नद्रौ कतिचिदबलाविप्रयुक्तः स कामी
नीत्वा मासान्कनकवलयभ्रंशरिक्तप्रकोष्ठः ।
आषाढस्य प्रथमदिवसे मेघमाश्लिष्टसानुं
वप्रक्रीडापरिणतगजप्रेक्षणीयं ददर्श ॥ २ ॥

तस्य स्थित्वा कथमपि पुरः कौतुगाधानहेतो-
रन्तर्बाष्पश्चिरमनुचरो राजराजस्य दध्यौ ।
मेघालोके भवति सुखिनोऽप्यन्यथावृत्ति चेतः
कण्ठाश्लेषप्रणयिनि जने किं पुनर्दूरसंस्थे ॥ ३ ॥

This Yaksha, banished a desolate year
from his love and from the king whose curse
for some carelessness sent him impotent away,
spent his exile among the holy retreats
of Rāmagiri where Sītā, bathing, had made
the waters holy and where trees cast a rich shade.

On this mountain, months from his mate,
aching for love, his wrist so wasted
that the gold bracelet he wore slipped off
and was lost—he saw at summer's end
a cloud swelling against the peak
like a great elephant nuzzling a hill.

So he stood there, shaken, this courtier
of Kubera, his tears held back, considering
that heart-breaking sight a long time.
A sudden cloud can mute the mind
of the happiest man—how much more
when the one he is dying to hold is far from him.

प्रत्यासन्ने नभसि दयिताजीवितालम्बनार्थीं
    जीमूतेन स्वकुशलमयीं हारयिष्यन्प्रवृत्तिम् ।
स प्रत्यग्रैः कुटजकुसुमैः कल्पितार्घाय तस्मै
    प्रीतः प्रीतिप्रमुखवचनं स्वागतं व्याजहार ॥ ४ ॥

धूमज्योतिः सलिलमरुतां संनिपातः क्व मेघः
    संदेशार्थाः क्व पटुकरणैः प्राणिभिः प्रापणीयाः ।
इत्यौत्सुक्यादपरिगणयन्गुह्यकस्तं ययाचे
    कामार्ता हि प्रकृतिकृपणाश्चेतनाचेतनेषु ॥ ५ ॥

जातं वंशे भुवनविदिते पुष्करावर्तकानां
    जानामि त्वां प्रकृतिपुरुषं कामरूपं मघोनः ।
तेनार्थित्वं त्वयि विधिवशादूरबन्धुर्गतोऽहं
    याच्ञा मोघा वरमधिगुणे नाधमे लब्धकामा ॥ ६ ॥

4

Knowing the rains were near, desperate to keep
his love alive and thinking this cloud
could carry her news of how he was—
he offered it fresh blossoms
of the kuṭaja and, gladdened now,
welcomed it with warm words.

5

What does a cloud—a mix of vapor,
flame, water, and wind—have to do with messages
made to be sent by beings fit to bear them?
But still the Yaksha implored it. Those
sick with desire can no longer tell
what will answer and what is dumb.

6

"I know you born of a famous race of clouds
called 'The Whirlpools' and high minister to Indra,
able to take any shape you will—so I
who am far from my love by a fatal order,
implore you. Better a futile prayer
to greatness than the full favor of boors.] *political?*

संतप्तानां त्वमसि शरणं तत्पयोद प्रियाया:
संदेशं मे हर धनपतिक्रोधविश्लेषितस्य ।
गन्तव्या ते वसतिरलका नाम यक्षेश्वराणां
बाह्योद्यानस्थितहरशिरश्चन्द्रिकाधौतहर्म्या ॥ ७ ॥

त्वामारूढं पवनपदवीमुद्गृहीतालकान्ता:
प्रेक्षिष्यन्ते पथिकवनिता: प्रत्ययादाश्वसन्त्य: ।
क: संनद्धे विरहविधुरां त्वय्युपेक्षेत जायां
न स्यादन्योऽप्यहमिव जनो य: पराधीनवृत्ति: ॥ ८ ॥

मन्दं मन्दं नुदति पवनश्चानुकूलो यथा त्वां
वामश्चायं नदति मधुरं चातकस्ते सगन्ध: ।
गर्भाधानक्षणपरिचयान्नूनमाबद्धमाला:
सेविष्यन्ते नयनसुभगं खे भवन्तं बलाका: ॥ ९ ॥

7

O Cloud, remedy for those fevered with pain,
carry a message for me who am cut off
from my love by the fury of Kubera. You must go
to a city called Alakā where the mansions of Yaksha lords
are rinsed by moonlight beamed from the brow
of Shiva, whose home is an outlying grove.

8

Women whose men travel far roads will look up,
brushing hair from their eyes to see you crossing
the sky, their hearts lifted remembering what
you bring. And what man, when you loom ready to rain,
would let his woman suffer apart?—unless
like me, his life waits on another's whim.

9

A furthering wind heads you urgently
in the true way, and on your left
your kin, the chātaka, sings gladly,   *bird who lives on raindrops*
and cranes, knowing now is the time
to mate, attend you wave after wave,
so good is the sight of you in heaven.

तां चावश्यं दिवसगणनातत्परामेकपत्नी-
	मव्यापन्नामविहतगतिर्द्रक्ष्यसि भ्रातृजायाम् ।
आशाबन्धः कुसुमसदृशं प्रायशो ह्यङ्गनानां
	सद्यः पाति प्रणयि हृदयं विप्रयोगे रुणाद्धि॥ १० ॥

कर्तुं यच्च प्रभवति मही मुच्छिलीन्ध्रामवन्ध्यां
	तच्छुत्वा ते श्रवणसुभगं गर्जितं मानसोत्काः ।
आ कैलासाद्बिसकिसलयच्छेदपाथेयवन्तः
	संपत्स्यन्ते नभसि भवतो राजहंसा सहायाः ॥ ११ ॥

आपृच्छस्व प्रियसखममुं तुङ्गमालिङ्ग्य शैलं
	वन्द्यैः पुंसां रघुपतिपदैरङ्कितं मेखलासु ।
काले काले भवति भवता यस्य संयोगमेत्य
	स्नेहव्यक्तिश्चिरविरहजं मुञ्चतो बाष्पमुष्णम् ॥ १२ ॥

10

And surely, your way all clear, you will see
your friend's woman, my single-minded
love, counting the days and enduring.
For the stem of hope most often holds up
a woman's loving heart like a blossom,
quick to wither when cut off.

11

And hearing as far away as Mount Kailāsa
thunder that comes to cover the yielding earth
with mushrooms—a sound sweet to their ears—
proud geese, longing to reach
Lake Mānasa and carrying lotus shoots
for food, will be, O Cloud, your companions.

12

With this embrace of your dear friend
whose slopes are printed with the adored steps
of the Lord of the Raghus, leave him,   *Rama*
this tall peak who every season, meeting
with you, shows the love that comes from long absence,
proven by the fall of warm tears.

मार्गं तावच्छृणु कथयतस्त्वत्प्रयाणानुरूपं
संदेशं मे तदनु जलद श्रोष्यसि श्रोत्रपेयम् ।
खिन्नः खिन्नः शिखरिषु पदं न्यस्त गन्तासि यत्र
क्षीणः क्षीणः परिलघु पयः स्रोतसां चोपभुज्य ॥ १३ ॥

अद्रेः शृङ्गं हरति पवनः किंस्विदित्युन्मुखीभि-
र्दृष्टोत्साहश्चकितचकितं मुग्धसिद्धाङ्गनाभिः ।
स्थानादस्मात्सरसनिचुलादुत्पतोदङ्मुखः खं
दिङ्नागानां पथि परिहरन्स्थूलहस्तावलेपान् ॥ १४ ॥

रत्नच्छायाव्यतिकर इव प्रेक्ष्यमेतत्पुरस्ता-
द्वल्मीकाग्रात्प्रभवति धनुःखण्डमाखण्डलस्य ।
येन श्यामं वपुरतितरां कान्तिमापत्स्यते ते
बर्हेणेव स्फुरितरुचिना गोपवेषस्य विष्णोः ॥ १५ ॥

13

But before you hear my pleasing message,
listen, Cloud, while I tell you now
the right way to go for your journey,
the road to pursue after you've paused
on mountains whenever weary or when,
worn out, you've drunk the fine water of streams.

14

Then soar up out of this place where the nichulas _reeds_
are soaked with dew, and head north, your coming beheld
by simple Siddha women who'll look up amazed,   _group of_
wondering if wind has made off with a mountain top.   _women_
But avoid on your path the proudly lifted trunks
of the elephant guards of the Eight Directions.

15

There, risen from the top of an anthill,
like a mingle of glittering gems, will be seen
above you a fragment of rainbow from which your body
takes on a marvelous grace like Vishṇu's
when he came as Krishṇa, a cowherd,
with the spread splendor of his peacock crest.

त्वय्यायत्तं कृषिफलमिति भ्रूविकारानभिज्ञैः
प्रीतिस्निग्धैर्जनपदवधूलोचनैः पीयमानः ।
सद्यःसीरोत्कषणसुरभि क्षेत्रमारुह्य मालं
किंचित्पश्चाद्व्रज लघुगतिर्भूय एवोत्तरेण ॥ १६ ॥

त्वामासारप्रशमितवनोपप्लवं साधु मूर्ध्ना
वक्ष्यत्यध्वश्रमपरिगतं सानुमानाम्रकूटः ।
न क्षुद्रोऽपि प्रथममसुकृतापेक्षया संश्रयाय
प्राप्ते मित्रे भवति विमुखः किं पुनर्यस्तथोच्चैः ॥ १७ ॥

छन्नोपान्तः परिणतफलद्योतिभिः काननाम्रै-
स्त्वय्यारूढे शिखरमचलः स्निग्धवेणीसवर्णे ।
नूनं यास्यत्यमरमिथुनप्रेक्षणीयामवस्थां
मध्ये श्यामः स्तन इव भुवः शेषविस्तारपाण्डुः ॥ १८ ॥

26

16

Drunk in by the eyes of country brides—
still innocent of flirting and moist with gladness
because the crop has waited for you—lift yourself
to high ground some distance to the west where the land,
freshly opened by plows, perfumes the air,
then move with a light stride still further north.

17

There, when you're tired, Mount Āmrakūṭa will bear you
gladly on his heights, you that have doused
his burning woods with showers. Even
someone low, remembering past favors,
will not turn his face away when a friend seeks shelter—
how much less he who is so lofty?

18

Its slopes covered by the glow of ripened mangos
and with you poised on its crest, darkly shining
like a braid of coiled hair, the mountain seems
a great breast of earth, dark at its center,
pale gold around, a vision
right for a loving pair of immortals.

स्थित्वा तस्मिन्वनचरवधूभुक्तकुञ्जे मुहूर्तं
    तोयोत्सर्गद्रुततरगतिस्तत्परं वर्त्म तीर्णः ।
रेवां द्रक्ष्यस्युपलविषमे विन्ध्यपादे विशीर्णां
    भक्तिच्छेदैरिव विरचितां भूतिमङ्गे गजस्य ॥ १६ ॥

तस्यास्तिक्तैर्वनगजमदैर्वासितं वान्तवृष्टि-
    जम्बूकुञ्जप्रतिहतरयं तोयमादाय गच्छेः ।
अन्तःसारं घन तुलयितुं नानिलः शक्ष्यति त्वां
    रिक्तः सर्वो भवति हि लघुः पूर्णता गौरवाय ॥ २० ॥

नीपं दृष्ट्वा हरितकपिशं केसरैरर्धरूढै-
    राविर्भूतप्रथममुकुलाः कन्दलीश्चानुकच्छम् ।
दग्धारण्येष्वधिकसुरभिं गन्धमाघ्राय चोर्व्याः
    सारङ्गास्ते जललवमुचः सूचयिष्यन्ति मार्गम् ॥ २१ ॥

19

Resting awhile on the mountain whose groves gladden
the wives of woodsmen, then crossing the road beyond it
at a faster pace, being light of water,
you'll see at the Vindhya's rock-jammed base
the river Revā whose stream is scattered like streaks
of ash daubed on an elephant's flanks.

20

Now you should move on, having dropped
your rain and drunk from that river whose flow
is choked with rose apples, whose waters taste
richly of rutting elephants. But now
the wind will be too weak to hoist you—the empty
is light; fullness makes for weight.

21

Seeing the nīpa's flowers mix orange
with green, petal with half-grown stamen,
and the kandalīs on every wet bank
just showing their buds, and catching the heady scent
of earth in the charred woods, the chātaka birds will mark
the track you take as you go shedding rain.

उत्पश्यामि द्रुतमपि सखे मत्प्रियार्थं यियासो:
	कालक्षेपं ककुभसुरभौ पर्वते पर्वते ते ।
शुक्लाङ्गैः सजलनयनैः स्वागतीकृत्य केका:
	प्रत्युद्यात: कथमपि भवानन्तुमाशु व्यवस्येत् ॥ २२ ॥

पाण्डुच्छायोपवनवृतय: केतकैः सूचिभिन्नै-
	र्नीडारम्भैर्गृहबलिभुजामाकुलग्रामचैत्या: ।
त्वय्यासन्ने परिणतफलश्यामजम्बूवनान्ता:
	संपत्स्यन्ते कतिपयदिनस्थायिहंसा दशार्णा: ॥ २३ ॥

तेषां दिक्षु प्रथितविदिशालक्षणां राजधानीं
	गत्वा सद्य: फलमविकलं कामुकत्वस्य लब्धा ।
तीरोपान्तस्तनितसुभगं पास्यसि स्वादु यत्त-
	त्सभ्रूभङ्गं मुखमिव पयो वेत्रवत्याश्चलोर्मि ॥ २४ ॥

22

I foresee, friend, that though you want to hurry
my message, there will be pause after pause
on each peak that blossoms with fragrant kakubhas,
and though peacocks, eyes moist with gladness,
make you welcome, their cries risen to meet you, I pray
you somehow find the will to move quickly on.

23

When you come to rest in the Dashārṇa country,
garden hedges will be white with ketaka flowers
opening at their tips, and the sacred trees
of its towns will clamor with crows building their nests,
its borders dark with ripened rose apples,
and geese will tarry there for days.

24

When you've come to the royal city, Vidishā, famous
everywhere, you'll get the whole fruit
of your thirsting desire, for you'll drink the savory water
of the Vetravatī, whose tide ripples
like bent brows in a face made lovely frowning
at your soft thunder along her banks.

नीचैराख्यं गिरिमधिवसेस्तत्र विश्रामहेतो-
　　स्त्वत्संपर्कात्पुलकितमिव प्रौढपुष्पैः कदम्बैः ।
यः पण्यस्त्रीरतिपरिमलोद्गारिभिर्नागराणा-
　　मुद्दामानि प्रथयति शिलावेश्मभिर्यौवनानि ॥ २५ ॥

विश्रान्तः सन्व्रज वननदीतीरजातानि सिञ्च-
　　न्नुद्यानानां नवजलकणैर्यूथिकाजालकानि ।
गण्डस्वेदापनयनरुजाक्लान्तकर्णोत्पलानां
　　छायादानात्क्षणपरिचितः पुष्पलावीमुखानाम् ॥ २६ ॥

वक्रः पन्था यदपि भवतः प्रस्थितस्योत्तराशां
　　सौधोत्सङ्गप्रणयविमुखो मा स्म भूरुज्जयिन्याः ।
विद्युद्दामस्फुरितचकितैस्तत्र पौराङ्गनानां
　　लोलापाङ्गैर्यदि न रमसे लोचनैर्वञ्चितोऽसि ॥ २७ ॥

32

25

You should pause for a rest on the low peak called Nīchais
where the kadambas will spring to full blossom
at your touch, like thrilled hair prickling with delight.
Its stone caves exhale the perfume
that bought women use for their loving, so the peak
accuses the wild young men of the town.

26

Rested now, go on, lightly shedding
fresh water on the masses of jasmine raised
on the banks of the woodland stream, touching a sweet moment
with your shade the faces of girls harvesting flowers,
who bruise the lotuses hung at their ears
each time they brush the sweat from their cheeks.

27

Though it takes you off your northward course,
don't neglect the view of the roofs
of Ujjayinī's white mansions. If you aren't delighted
here in the women's eyes—their darting
sidelong looks startled by the glitter
of your cleft lightning—why, you have been cheated.

वीचिक्षोभस्तनितविहगश्रेणिकाञ्चीगुणायाः
संसर्पन्त्याः स्खलितसुभगं दर्शितावर्तनाभेः ।
निर्विन्ध्यायाः पथि भव रसाभ्यन्तरः संनिपत्य
स्त्रीणामाद्यं प्रणयवचनं विभ्रमो हि प्रियेषु ॥ २८ ॥

वेणीभूतप्रतनुसलिला तामतीतस्य सिन्धुः
पाण्डुच्छाया तटरुहतरुभ्रंशिभिर्जीर्णपर्णैः ।
सौभाग्यं ते सुभग विरहावस्थया व्यञ्जयन्ती
कार्श्यं येन त्यजति विधिना स त्वयैवोपपाद्यः ॥ २९ ॥

प्राप्यावन्तीनुदयनकथाकोविदग्रामवृद्धा-
न्पूर्वोद्दिष्टामनुसर पुरीं श्रीविशालां विशालाम् ।
स्वल्पीभूते सुचरितफले स्वर्गिणां गां गतानां
शेषैः पुण्यैर्हृतमिव दिवः कान्तिमत्खण्डमेकम् ॥ ३० ॥

28

On your way, when you meet the Nirvindhyā River,
whose stumbling glide is filled with grace, whose eddies
make her a navel, whose belt is a clamoring row
of birds on her swaying billows—be sure you fill yourself
with her waters, for the first show of women's love
for their favorites is surely in tempting play.

29

Crossing the Sindhu, you'll have to do
whatever you can to make the river stop
her wasting away—a sign of your good luck—lovesick
and pitiable with your absence. Her thinned current
is a single braid of hair, her wanness
faded leaves fallen from the trees on her banks.

30

Reaching Avantī whose old countrymen know
Udayana's story by heart, seek out the city
whose riches I've mentioned, Vishālā,
like a lovely piece of heaven brought down by the left-
over grace of those who achieved a divine home
but, their merit dwindling, came back to earth.

दीर्घीकुर्वन्पटु मदकलं कूजितं सारसानां
प्रत्यूषेषु स्फुटितकमलामोदमैत्रीकषाय: ।
यत्र स्त्रीणां हरति सुरतग्लानिमङ्गानुकूल:
शिप्रावात: प्रियतम इव प्रार्थनाचाटुकार: ॥ ३१ ॥

जालोद्गीर्णैरुपचितवपु: केशसंस्कारधूपै-
र्बन्धुप्रीत्या भवनशिखिभिर्दत्तनृत्तोपहार: ।
हर्म्येष्वस्या: कुसुमसुरभिष्वध्वखिन्नान्तरात्मा
नीत्वा रात्रि ललितवनितापादरागाङ्कितेषु ॥ ३२ ॥

भर्तु: कण्ठच्छविरिति गणै: सादरं वीक्ष्यमाण:
पुण्यं यायास्त्रिभुवनगुरोर्धाम चण्डीश्वरस्य ।
धूतोद्यानं कुवलयरजोगन्धिभिर्गन्धवत्या-
स्तोयक्रीडानिरतयुवतिस्नानतिक्तैर्मरुद्भि: ॥ ३३ ॥

31

There, the breeze at sunrise blowing
from the Shiprā River, prolonging the blurred
piercing cries of passionate cranes, is filled
with the fragrance of the lotus blossoms it fondles
and, soothing the skin, arouses sleepy
satisfied women like a lover coaxing to love-play.

32

Incense women use to perfume their hair,
drifting up through latticed windows, will swell
your form, and your friends the peacocks will offer their dancing
for welcome. So, worn with travel, pass the night
at palaces scented with flowers and stained
with red lac from the lovely feet of girls.

33

And you must visit there the only shrine
of the Master of the Three Worlds, Chaṇḍī's Lord,
His groves ruffled by breezes from the Gandhavatī,
heavy with pollen and fragrant from the perfume of girls
at play in the water. There, Shiva's attendants amazed
at your sight, will see in your hue the dark of their own Lord's throat.

अप्यन्यस्मिञ्जलधर महाकालमासाद्य काले
स्थातव्यं ते नयनविषयं यावदत्येति भानुः ।
कुर्वन्संध्याबलिपटहतां शूलिनः श्लाघनीया-
मामन्द्राणां फलमविकलं लप्स्यसे गर्जितानाम् ॥ ३४ ॥

पादन्यासैः क्वणितरशनास्तत्र लीलावधूतै
रत्नच्छायाखचितवलिभिश्चामरैः क्लान्तहस्ताः ।
वेश्यास्त्वत्तो नखपदसुखान्प्राप्य वर्षाग्रबिन्दू-
नामोक्ष्यन्ते त्वचि मधुकरश्रेणिदीर्घान्कटाक्षान् ॥ ३५ ॥

पश्चादुच्चैर्भुजतरुवनं मण्डलेनाभिलीनः
सांध्यं तेजः प्रतिनवजपापुष्परक्तं दधानः ।
नृत्तारम्भे हर पशुपतेरार्द्रनागाजिनेच्छां
शान्तोद्वेगस्तिमितनयनं दृष्टभक्तिर्भवान्या ॥ ३६ ॥

34

O Cloud, being in Mahākāla
then, though it's early still, you should rest
until the sun sets, and then perform
the high office of drum for the Lord's
twilight service, and you will receive
the full reward of your mellow thunder.

35

The dancing girls there, belts clinking
as they place their feet, weary hands elegantly
flicking those fly whisks with gem-studded handles,
feeling your first drops so soothing
to scratched skin, will send you, like a flight
of bees, long sidling looks.

36

Then, resting as a sphere on the tall forest
of Shiva's arms, and taking luster from the twilight—
red as just-blooming china roses—offer yourself
to Shiva for the elephant's bloody hide
He wears in His dance, your devotion observed
by Bhavānī with steady eyes, her terror now calmed.

गच्छन्तीनां रमणवसतिं योषितां तत्र नक्तं
रुद्धालोके नरपतिपथे सूचिभेद्यैस्तमोभिः ।
सौदामन्या कनकनिकषस्निग्धया दर्शयोर्वीं
तोयोत्सर्गस्तनितमुखरो मा च भूर्विक्लवास्ताः ॥ ३७ ॥

तां कस्यांचिद्भुवनवलभौ सुप्तपारावतायां
नीत्वा रात्रिं चिरविलसनात्खिन्नविद्युत्कलत्रः ।
दृष्टे सूर्ये पुनरपि भवान्वाहयेदध्वशेषं
मन्दायन्ते न खलु सुहृदामभ्युपेतार्थकृत्याः ॥ ३८ ॥

तस्मिन्काले नयनसलिलं योषितां खण्डितानां
शान्तिं नेयं प्रणयिभिरतो वर्त्म भानोस्त्यजाशु ।
प्रालेयास्त्रं कमलवदनात्सोऽपि हर्तुं नलिन्याः
प्रत्यावृत्तस्त्वयि कररुधि स्यादनल्पाभ्यसूयः ॥ ३६ ॥

37

There, with the gleam of your lightning like a gold streak
on a touchstone, you'll show the path by night
to young women on their way to love
when the king's highway is muffled in so thick
a dark a pin could pierce it. But don't thunder
or pour down rain, for they are timid things.

38

After a night on some ridged roof
where pigeons sleep and your mate, the lightning,
is played out with love's repeated flashes,
the sun will rise and you must make ready, O Cloud,
to finish your journey. Those who work
for the good of their friends don't waste time.

39

It's now that the tears of jealous girls
are smoothed away by lovers. So it's best
you hurry out of the sun's path, for he also
returns to wipe away the tears of dew
from the face of the lotus and will be furious
if you hinder the reach of his rays.

गम्भीराया: पयसि सरितश्चेतसीव प्रसन्ने
  छायात्माऽपि प्रकृतिसुभगो लप्स्यते ते प्रवेशम् ।
तस्मादस्या: कुमुदविशदान्यर्हसि त्वं न धैर्या-
  न्मोघीकर्तुं चटुलशफरोद्वर्तनप्रेक्षितानि ॥ ४० ॥

तस्या: किंचित्करधृतमिव प्राप्तवानीरशाखं
  हृत्वा नीलं सलिलवसनं मुक्तरोधोनितम्बम् ।
प्रस्थानं ते कथमपि सखे लम्बमानस्य भावि
  ज्ञातास्वादो विवृतजघनां को विहातुं समर्थ: ॥ ४१ ॥

त्वन्निष्यन्दोच्छ्वसितवसुधागन्धसंपर्करम्य:
  स्रोतोरन्ध्रध्वनितसुभगं दन्तिभि: पीयमान: ।
नीचैर्वास्यत्युपजिगमिषोर्देवपूर्वं गिरिं ते
  शीतो वायु: परिणमयिता काननोदुम्बराणाम् ॥ ४२ ॥

40

Handsome by nature, you'll find a way
into the waters of the Gambhīrā,
as into a clear heart, with your reflection,
so don't from simple stubbornness
dismiss her glances—those flirting leaps
of shaphara fish, white as lotuses.

41

You'll snatch off her blue gown of water,
which will slide to her hips so that cane branches
on the banks will seem like hands
clutching what's left, and, friend,
it won't be so easy to leave, as you cling
to her still. What lover, done with loving,
can leave a girl with her lap laid bare?

42

As you drift on to Devagiri,
a cool wind, ripener of figs,
will urge you gently from below,
fragrant from sweeping the earth soaked
with your showers and drunk in by elephants
who inhale with a pleasing thunder.

तत्र स्कन्दं नियतवसति पुष्पमेघीकृतात्मा
पुष्पासारैः स्नपयतु भवान्व्योमगङ्गाजलार्द्रैः ।
रक्षाहेतोर्नवशशिभृता वासवीनां चमूना-
मत्यादित्यं हुतवहमुखे संभृतं तद्धि तेजः ॥ ४३ ॥

ज्योतिर्लेखावलयि गलितं यस्य बर्हं भवानी
पुत्रप्रेम्णा कुवलयदलप्रापि कर्णे करोति ।
धौतापाङ्गं हरशशिरुचा पावकेस्तं मयूरं
पश्चादद्रिग्रहणगुरुभिर्गर्जितैर्नर्तयेथाः ॥ ४४ ॥

आराध्यैनं शरणवभवं देवमुल्लङ्घिताध्वा
सिद्धद्वन्द्वैर्जलकणभयाद्वीणिभिर्मुक्तमार्गः ।
व्यालम्बेथाः सुरभितनयालम्भजां मानयिष्य-
न्स्रोतोमूर्त्या भुवि परिणतां रन्तिदेवस्य कीर्तिम् ॥ ४५ ॥

43

There, forming into a cloud full of flowers,
you must rain down on Skanda whose home this is—
a burst of blossoms moistened by the heavenly Gaṅgā—
because he is that radiant seed surpassing the sun
and put by Shiva—crested with the new moon—
in Agni's mouth to protect the armies of Indra.

44

Then, with your thunder doubled by its own echo
from the mountain, you should make Skanda's peacock dance,
the corners of its eyes bright with the gleam of Hara's moon—
that peacock whose feather with its fire-streaked circles,
Bhavānī, for love of her son, sets at her ear,
where it hangs down smartly on the blue lotus petal there.

45

So this much of your journey past, done
with adoring the god born in the reeds, while pairs
of Siddhas shun your path, fearing the harm
your rain might do to their lutes, you should now descend
to honor the famous offering of Rantideva,
those cows transformed to a river here on earth.

त्वय्यादातुं जलमवनते शाङ्‌र्गिणो वर्णचौरे
तस्या: सिन्धो: पृथुमपि तनुं दूरभावात्प्रवाहम् ।
प्रेक्षिष्यन्ते गगनगतयो नूनमावर्ज्य दृष्टी-
रेकं मुक्तागुणमिव भुव: स्थूलमध्येन्द्रनीलम् ॥ ४६ ॥

तामुत्तीर्य व्रज परिचितभ्रूलताविभ्रमाणां
पक्ष्मोत्क्षेपादुपरिविलसत्कृष्णशारप्रभाणाम् ।
कुन्दक्षेपानुगममधुकरश्रीमुषामात्मबिम्बं
पात्रीकुर्वन्दशपुरवधूनेत्रकौतूहलानाम् ॥ ४७ ॥

ब्रह्मावर्तं जनपदमधश्छायया गाहमान:
क्षेत्रं क्षत्रप्रधनपिशुनं कौरवं तद्‌भजेथा: ।
राजन्यानां शितशरशतैर्यत्र गाण्डीवधन्वा
धारापातैस्त्वमिव कमलान्यभ्यवर्षन्मुखानि ॥ ४८ ॥

46

When you descend with Krishṇa's color,
to drink its waters, all the wanderers
of heaven will see from far off
the river's flow—even though broad—
as narrow, as if a strand of pearls
had a thick sapphire at its middle.

47

Crossing that river, you must go on and make yourself
something to wonder at for Dashapura's women,
whose eyes know well the play of the full brow
and whose pupils, darkly radiant, flare upward
when their lashes lift, stealing the beauty
of black bees on swaying white jasmine.

48

With your shadow, down below, falling across
the country of the Brahmāvarta,
you should go to the field of the Kurus,
renowned as the battleground where Arjuna
showered his sharp arrows on princely chests,
as you pour jets of water on the lotus.

हित्वा हालामभिमतरसां रेवतीलोचनाङ्कां
    बन्धुप्रीत्या समरविमुखो लाङ्गली याः सिषेवे ।
कृत्वा तासामधिगममपां सौम्य सारस्वतीना-
    मन्तः शुद्धस्त्वमपि भविता वर्णमात्रेण कृष्णः ॥ ४६ ॥

तस्मादगच्छेरनुकनखलं शैलराजावतीर्णां
    जाह्नोः कन्यां सगरतनयस्वर्गसोपानपङ्क्तिम् ।
गौरीवक्त्रभ्रुकुटिरचनां या विहस्येव फेनैः
    शंभोः केशग्रहणमकरोदिन्दुलग्नोर्मिहस्ता ॥ ५० ॥

तस्या पातुं सुरगज इव व्योम्नि पश्चार्धलम्बी
    त्वं चेदच्छस्फटिकविशदं तर्केयेस्तिर्यगम्भः !
संसर्पन्त्या सपदि भवतः स्रोतसि च्छाययाऽसौ
    स्यादस्थानोपगतयमुनासंगमेवाभिरामा ॥ ५१ ॥

49

The same waters of the Sarasvatī, that Balarāma,
loving his friends too much to fight them,
took in place of the savory wine that reflected
his dear Revatī's eyes—this same water,
serving you well—will cleanse you, friend,
leaving you dark only in hue.

50

From there you should go to Jahnu's daughter who descends
from the Lord of the Peaks near Mount Kanakhala
and once served Sagara's sons as a stairway to heaven.
It was she, Gangā, her foam like laughter
at Gaurī's frown, who grabbed at Shiva's hair,
her waves hands that reached to His crowning moon.

51

If it's her waters, clear as unclouded crystal,
you aim to drink like an elephant of the gods,
hanging from your hindquarters down from heaven and angled
into her drift, she—suddenly so lovely
with your reflection in her current—may seem
to have joined the Yamunā at the wrong place.

आसीनानां सुरभितशिलं नाभिगन्धैर्मृगाणां
तस्या एव प्रभवमचलं प्राप्य गौरं तुषारैः ।
वक्ष्यस्यध्वश्रमविनयने तस्य शृङ्गे निषण्णः
शोभां शुभ्रत्रिनयनवृषोत्खातपङ्कोपमेयाम् ॥ ५२ ॥

तं चेद्वायौ सरति सरलस्कन्धसघट्टजन्मा
बाधेतोल्काक्षपितचमरीबालभारो दवाग्निः ।
अर्हस्येनं शमयितुमलं वारिधारासहस्रै—
रापन्नार्तिप्रशमनफलाः संपदो ह्युत्तमानाम् ॥ ५३ ॥

ये संरम्भोत्पतनरभसाः स्वाङ्गभङ्गाय तस्मि—
न्मुक्ताध्वानं सपदि शरभा लङ्घयेयुर्भवन्तम् ।
तान्कुर्वीथास्तुमुलकरकावृष्टिहासावकीर्णा—
न्के वा न स्युः परिभवपदं निष्फलारम्भयत्नाः ॥ ५४ ॥

52

Now, up on that height which fathers
this very stream—pale under snow and with rocks
perfumed by the musk deer sitting on them—
you'll assume, as you rest on its peak to gather strength,
a beauty like the mud churned up
by the white bull of the Triple-eyed God.

53

If, when the wind rises, fire should threaten,
spreading from friction in the crowns of long-needled pines,
spark showers burning the thick tails of yaks,
you must snuff it with a thousand water spouts,
since the good of a great man's fortune is found
in softening the pain of the oppressed.

54

In their rage furiously lunging up
only to wound themselves, the sharabhas
might suddenly attack you there, maddened
by the discharge of your thunder. You should scatter them
with a laughing volley of hard hail. What man
isn't thought a fool who works to no end?

तत्र व्यक्तं दृषदि चरणन्यासमर्धेन्दुमौले:
शश्वत्सिद्धैरुपहृतबलि भक्तिनम्र: परीया: ।
यस्मिन्दृष्टे करणविगमादूर्ध्वमुद्धूतपापा:
कल्पन्तेऽस्य स्थिरगणपदप्राप्तये श्रद्दधाना: ॥ ५५ ॥

शब्दायन्ते मधुरमनिलै: कीचका: पूर्यमाणाः
संरक्ताभिस्त्रिपुरविजयो गीयते किंनरीभि: ।
निर्ह्रादी ते मुरज इव चेत्कन्दरेषु ध्वनि: स्या-
त्संगीतार्थो ननु पशुपतेस्तत्र भावी समस्त: ॥ ५६ ॥

प्रालेयाद्रेरुपतटमतिक्रम्य तांस्तान्विशेषा–
न्हंसद्वारं भृगपतिशयोवर्त्म यत्क्रौञ्चरन्ध्रम् ।
तेनोदीचीं दिशमनुसरेस्तिर्यगायामशोभी
श्याम: पादो बलिनियमनाभ्युद्यतस्येव विष्णो: ॥ ५७ ॥

55

There, bent with reverence, you must circle
the footprint of mooncrested Shiva, stamped clearly
in the stone and always heaped with offerings
of Siddhas. The faithful by seeing it merely
are purged of sins and become, when their bodies
fall away, His eternal attendants.

56

Bamboos, filling with wind, cry sweetly,
and the divine women of the Kinnaras
chant in full accord the conquest
of Tripura. If your thunder, rumbling
in the caves, should sound like a tabor, the music
for the Lord of Beasts will truly be perfect.

57

Having passed over many marvels on the slopes
of Himālaya, you must move on northward by way
of the gate of geese and then the road to glory
for the Bhrigu's lord—that chasm in Mount Krauncha—
stretching your length through, till you seem like Vishṇu's
dark foot about to step on Bali.

गत्वा चोर्ध्वं दशमुखभुजोच्छ्वासितप्रस्थसंधे:
कैलासस्य त्रिदशवनितादर्पणस्यातिथि: स्या: ।
शृङ्गोच्छ्रायै: कुमुदविशदैर्यो वितत्य स्थित: खं
राशीभूत: प्रतिदिनमिव त्र्यम्बकस्याट्टहास: ॥ ५८ ॥

उत्पश्यामि त्वयि तटगते स्निग्धभिन्नाञ्जनाभे
सद्य:कृत्तद्विरददशनच्छेदगौरस्य तस्य ।
लीलामद्रे: स्तिमितनयनप्रेक्षणीयां भवित्री-
मंसन्यस्ते सति हलभृतो मेचके वाससीव ॥ ५९ ॥

हित्वा तस्मिन्भुजगवलयं शंभुना दत्तहस्ता
क्रीडाशैले यदि च विचरेत्पादचारेण गौरी ।
भङ्गीभक्त्या विरचितवपु: स्तम्भितान्तर्जलौघ:
सोपानत्वं कुरु मणितटारोहणायाग्रयायी ॥ ६० ॥

58

And lifting still higher, you should be welcomed
by Kailāsa—the mirror for goddesses—
the joints of its peaks cracked by Rāvaṇa's arms,
as it spreads its crests across the sky
like a field of white lotuses, as though the laughing
of Shiva were heaped up day after day.

59

I can foresee that when you—looking like collyrium
made shiny dark from grinding—rest on its slopes
white as new-cut ivory, the mountain,
like Balarāma when he sets
his black mantle on his shoulders,
will draw to itself steady-eyed looks with its grace.

60

And if Gaurī, her hand held by Shiva
who has tossed aside His armlet of snakes,
should stroll on that pleasure mount, you must make yourself
into a flight of stairs—your inward waters
hardened to wavelike steps—and go
before her as she climbs its jeweled slopes.

तत्रावश्यं वलयकुलिशोद्धट्टनोद्गीर्णतोयं
नेष्यन्ति त्वां सुरयुवतयो यन्त्रधारागृहत्वम् ।
ताभ्यो मोक्षस्तव यदि सखे धर्मलब्धस्य न स्या-
त्क्रीडालोला: श्रवणपरुषैर्गर्जितैर्भाययेस्ता: ॥ ६१ ॥

हेमाम्भोजप्रसवि सलिलं मानसस्यादददान:
कुर्वन्कामात्क्षणमुखपटप्रीतिमैरावणस्य ।
धुन्वन्वातै: सजलपृषतै: कल्पवृक्षांशुकानि
छायाभिन्न: स्फटिकविशदं निर्विशेस्तं नगेन्द्रम् ॥ ६२ ॥

तस्योत्सङ्गे प्रणयिन इव स्रस्तगङ्गादुकूलां
न त्वं दृष्ट्वा न पुनरलकां ज्ञास्यसे कामचारिन् ।
या व: काले वहति सलिलोद्गारमुच्चैर्विमाना
मुक्ताजालग्रथितमलकं कामिनीवाभ्रवृन्दम् ॥ ६३ ॥

61

Here heavenly girls will surely
use you for their bath, your showers
released by the scratching of their gemmed bracelets,
and friend, if you can't free yourself from them
in the hot season, you should scare them
with your rough thunder while they're deep in their play.

62

Taking the waters of Lake Mānasa, nurse
to the golden lotus, you can please Airāvata awhile
by lending his face cover, then with squally breezes
shake the garments hung on the Wishing Tree
and enjoy the Lord of Heights, your shadow
making a second self on his bright crystals.

63

Seeing my city again—the Gangā seeming a gown
that slips off it as though it sat
on a lover's lap—you'll have no trouble, moving
at your own pleasure, knowing Alakā
which hefts, with its high mansions, masses
of clouds spilling their rain in your season,
like a woman whose hair is bound up by strings of pearls.

विद्युत्वन्तं ललितवनिताः सेन्द्रचापं सचित्राः
संगीताय प्रहतमुरजाः स्निग्धगम्भीरघोषम् ।
अन्तस्तोयं मणिमयभुवस्तुङ्गमभ्रंलिहाग्राः
प्रासादास्त्वां तुलयितुमलं यत्र तैस्तैर्विशेषैः ॥ ६४ ॥

हस्ते लीलाकमलमलके बालकुन्दानुविद्धं
नीता लोध्रप्रसवरजसा पाण्डुतामानने श्रीः ।
चूडापाशे नवकुरवकं चारु कर्णे शिरीषं
सीमन्ते च त्वदुपगमजं यत्र नीपं वधूनाम् ॥ ६५ ॥

यस्यां यक्षाः सितमणिमयान्येत्य हर्म्यस्थलानि
ज्योतिश्छायाकुसुमरचितान्युत्तमस्त्रीसहायाः ।
आसेवन्ते मधु रतिफलं कल्पवृक्षप्रसूतं
त्वद्गम्भीरध्वनिषु शनकैः पुष्करेष्वाहतेषु ॥ ६६ ॥

64

Its mansions are your equals—they have for your lightning
the flash of dazzling women, for your rainbow
arrays of paintings, for your deep and soothing thunder
drums beating for dance and song, for your core
of waters floors inset with gems, and roofs
that graze the sky for your loftiness.

65

There, the hands of girls toy with lotuses,
their curls woven with new jasmine, the beauty
of their faces made fairer by pollen from the lodhra tree,
their crowning braids full of the fresh crimson amaranth,
sweet shirīshas at their ears, and the nīpa blossom
that springs up to your coming, set in the part of their hair.

66

There, Yakshas, who come with most lovely companions
to the palace roofs whose flowers are stars
reflected from crystal floors, enjoy
the wine that arouses love, a gift
from the Wishing Tree, while drums are sounded
gently like your deep thunders.

यत्र स्त्रीणां प्रियतमभुजोच्छ्वासितालिङ्गिताना-
मङ्गग्लानि सुरतजनितां तन्तुजालावलम्बाः ।
त्वत्संरोधापगमविशदश्चन्द्रपादैर्निशीथे
व्यालुम्पन्ति स्फुटजललवस्यन्दिनश्चन्द्रकान्ताः ॥ ६७ ॥

नेत्रा नीताः सततगतिना यद्विमानाग्रभूमी-
रालेख्यानां सलिलकणिकादोषमुत्पाद्य सद्यः ।
शङ्काास्पृष्टा इव जलमुचस्त्वादृशा जालमार्गै-
र्धूमोद्गारानुकृतिनिपुणा जर्जरा निष्पतन्ति ॥ ६८ ॥

नीवीबन्धोच्छ्वसितशिथिलं यत्र बिम्बाधराणां
क्षौमं रागादनिभृतकरेष्वाक्षिपत्सु प्रियेषु ।
अर्चिस्तुङ्गानभिमुखमपि प्राप्य रत्नप्रदीपान्
ह्रीमूढानां भवति विफलप्रेरणा चूर्णमुष्टिः ॥ ६९ ॥

60

67

There—hung from a web of threads—
moonstones, at midnight shedding water in great drops
full of light because you have freed
the moon's rays, wholly dispel the drowse
of women exhausted by pleasure and lying
in the slack arms of the ones they love.

68

There, clouds like you, driven on
by the thrust of wind to the upper stories
of mansions, marring their paintings
with moisture, fly—as if suddenly afraid—
out the latticed windows in ragged shreds,
clever at aping puffs of smoke.

69

There, when the knots and clasps on the garments
of Yaksha women begin to come loose,
and lover's hands, ruthless from passion,
snatch off silks, the women are fuddled with shame
in the high glow of jewels that serve as lamps,
and fling handfuls of incense against them—in vain.

गत्युत्कम्पादलकपतितैर्यत्र मन्दारपुष्पै:
    पत्रच्छेदै: कनककमलै: कर्णविभ्रंशिभिश्च ।
मुक्ताजालै: स्तनपरिसरच्छिन्नसूत्रैश्च हारै-
    र्नैशो मार्ग: सवितुरुदये सूच्यते कामिनीनाम् ॥ ७० ॥

मत्वा देवं धनपतिसखं यत्र साक्षाद्वसन्तं
    प्रायश्चापं न वहति भयान्मन्मथ: षट्पदज्यम् ।
सभ्रूभङ्गप्रहितनयनै: कामिलक्ष्येष्वमोघै-
    स्तस्यारम्भश्चतुरवनिताविभ्रमैरेव सिद्ध: ॥ ७१ ॥

तत्रागारं धनपतिगृहानुत्तरेणास्मदीयं
    दूराल्लक्ष्यं सुरपतिधनुश्चारुणा तोरणेन ।
यस्योपान्ते कृतकतनय: कान्तया वर्धितो मे
    हस्तप्राप्यस्तबकनमितो बालमन्दारवृक्ष: ॥ ७२ ॥

70

There, the nightly path of loving girls
can be traced at sunup where their hurried steps
have left behind them coral blossoms fallen
from curls, fragments of golden lotus shed
from the ears, and necklaces of strung pearls,
their threads snapped just where they lie on the breast.

71

Knowing that Shiva Himself lives there,
the God of Love—wary of Him—
seldom carries his bee-strung bow,
his job done for him by the art
of clever girls whose eyes under arched brows
riddle their target lovers with lethal looks.

72

There, north of Kubera's estates, is our house,
visible from far off because its gate arches
brilliantly up like a rainbow, and on our grounds
a young Mandāra tree, bent by clusters
of bloom so the hand can reach them, is tended—
a sort of proxy son—by my love.

वापी चास्मिन्मरकतशिलाबद्धसोपानमार्गा
    हैमैश्छन्ना विकचकमलैः स्निग्धवैदूर्यनालैः ।
यस्यास्तोये कृतवसतयो मानसं संनिकृष्टं
    नाध्यास्यन्ति व्यपगतशुचस्त्वामपि प्रेक्ष्य हंसाः ॥ ७३ ॥

तस्यास्तीरे रचितशिखरः पेशलैरिन्द्रनीलैः
    क्रीडाशैलः कनककदलीवेष्टनप्रेक्षणीयः ।
मद्गेहिन्याः प्रिय इति सखे चेतसा कातरेण
    प्रेक्ष्योपान्तस्फुरिततडितं त्वां तमेव स्मरामि ॥ ७४ ॥

रक्ताशोकश्चलकिसलयः केसरश्चात्र कान्तः
    प्रत्याह्नौ कुरवककृतेर्माधवीमण्डपस्य ।
एकः सख्यास्तव सह मया वामपादाभिलाषी
    काङ्क्षत्यन्यो वदनमदिरां दोहदच्छद्मनास्याः ॥ ७५ ॥

73

There, too, is an oblong pool, its stairway shaped
of emerald slabs, its surface brimmed with full-blown
golden lotuses, their stalks glossy
as lapis lazuli. And, living in its water,
geese, their distress softened, forget—merely
by seeing you—their hunger for nearby Lake Mānasa.

74

By its edge there is a pleasure hill,
its crest devised of gorgeous sapphires
and beautifully hedged by golden plantains.
Seeing you, my friend, surrounded by lightning,
I remember it now—a favorite place
of my love—and my heart is shaken.

75

On it stands a ruddy ashoka, its branches
swaying, and a lovely kesara tree near the bower
of mādhavī vines bordered with red amaranth,
the first tree craving, as I do, the feel
of your friend's left foot, the second wine from her mouth,
pretending they need these to bring them to blossom.

तन्मध्ये च स्फटिकफलका काञ्चनी वासयष्टि––
मूले बद्धा मणिभिरनतिप्रौढवंशप्रकाशैः ।
तालैः शिञ्जावलयसुभगैर्नर्तितः कान्तया मे
यामध्यास्ते दिवसविगमे नीलकण्ठः सुहृद्वः ॥ ७६ ॥

एभिः साधो हृदयनिहितैर्लक्षणैर्लक्षयेथा
द्वारोपान्ते लिखितवपुषौ शङ्खपद्मौ च दृष्ट्वा ।
क्षामच्छायं भवनमधुना मद्वियोगेन नूनं
सूर्यापाये न खलु कमलं पुष्यति स्वामभिख्याम् ॥ ७७ ॥

गत्वा सद्यः कलभतनुतां शीघ्रसंपातहेतोः
क्रीडाशैले प्रथमकथिते रम्यसानौ निषण्ण ।
अर्हस्यन्तर्भवनपतितां कर्तुमल्पाल्पभासं
खद्योतालीविलसितनिभां विद्युदुन्मेषदृष्टिम् ॥ ७८ ॥

66

76

Between these, there's a golden perch,
its base, crystal inset with gems,
glowing like young bamboo. On it
your friend the peacock alights at the end
of day and dances to the pretty clink
of my darling's bangles as she claps the time.

77

With these signs stored in your heart,
Wise One, and seeing on the sides of the gate
two painted figures, a conch and a lotus,
you'll find my house, now surely
lusterless with my absence. The lotus
loses its aura when the sun is gone.

78

Small as a young elephant now
for a quick descent to that pleasure hill
we spoke of, and settling on its dazzling crest,
you should flash your glance—the lightning—
into the house, but most gently,
like the playful glow of a line of fireflies.

तन्वी श्यामा शिखरिदशना पक्वबिम्बाधरोष्ठी
    मध्ये क्षामा चकितहरिणीप्रेक्षणा निम्ननाभिः ।
श्रोणीभारादलसगमना स्तोकनम्रा स्तनाभ्यां
    या तत्र स्याद्युवतिविषये सृष्टिराद्येव धातुः ॥ ७९ ॥

तां जानीथाः परिमितकथां जीवितं मे द्वितीयं
    दूरीभूते मयि सहचरे चक्रवाकीमिवैकाम् ।
गाढोत्कण्ठां गुरुषु दिवसेष्वेषु गच्छत्सु बालां
    जातां मन्ये शिशिरमथितां पद्मिनीं वाऽन्यरूपाम् ॥ ८० ॥

नूनं तस्याः प्रबलरुदितोच्छूननेत्रं प्रियाया
    निःश्वासानामशिशिरतया भिन्नवर्णाधरोष्ठम् ।
हस्तन्यस्तं मुखमसकलव्यक्ति लम्बालकत्वा-
    दिन्दोर्दैन्यं त्वदनुसरणक्लिष्टकान्तेर्बिभर्ति ॥ ८१ ॥

79

There, you'll see a slim young girl, her teeth
pointed, her lower lip a bimba fruit,
small in the waist, eyes like a timid deer's,
her navel deep, her gait slowed by full hips,
her breasts bending her a little forward, she
who seems among women the first work of the Creator.

80

In her, who is so quiet, you should see—
I being far off—my second life,
a lonely chakravākī. I think
that young girl, deep in her longing
while these heavy days pass, must lose
her bloom like a lotus hurt by frost.

81

Surely, eyes swollen by continual tears,
lower lip faded by parching sighs,
my love's face, cupped in her hand
and partly hid by the fall of tangled hair,
bears a likeness to the miserable moon,
its splendor dimmed by your dark interruption.

आलोके ते निपतति पुरा सा बलिव्याकुला वा
मत्सादृश्यं विरहतनु वा भावगम्यं लिखन्ती ।
पृच्छन्ती वा मधुरवचनां सारिकां पञ्जरस्थां
कच्चिद्भर्तुः स्मरसि रसिके त्वं हि तस्य प्रियेति ॥ ८२ ॥

उत्सङ्गे वा मलिनवसने सौम्य निक्षिप्य वीणां
मद्गोत्राङ्कं विरचितपदं गेयमुद्गातुकामा ।
तन्त्रीमार्द्रां नयनसलिलैः सारयित्वा कथंचि-
द्भूयो भूयः स्वयमपि कृतां मूर्च्छनां विस्मरन्ती ॥ ८३ ॥

शेषान्मासान्विरहदिवसस्थापितस्यावधेर्वा
विन्यस्यन्ती भुवि गणनया देहलीदत्तपुष्पैः ।
संभोगं वा हृदयनिहितारम्भमास्वादयन्ती
प्रायेणैते रमणविरहेष्वङ्गनानां विनोदाः ॥ ८४ ॥

70

82

She will come into your view busy
at her worship or sketching me—
as she guesses—wasted by separation,
or asking the lyric sarikā
in its cage: 'O sweet bird, do you
remember the master? — for you were his favorite.'

83

Or setting the lute in her lap on her soiled gown,
because, O Gentle One, she wants to sing a song
whose words are arranged with my name as its burden,
somehow getting it tuned, its strings damp
with water from her eyes, but over and over
forgetting the tune though she herself composed it.

84

Or arranging flowers on the ground, placed
at the threshold, so she can count the months that remain
of the time set from the day of parting, or,
in her imaginings, living our pleasure
in love—for these are the usual ways
of killing time for women far from their mates.

सव्यापारामहनि न तथा पीडयेद्विप्रयोगः
शङ्के रात्रौ गुरुतरशुचं निर्विनोदां सखीं ते ।
मत्संदेशः सुखयितुमलं पश्य साध्वीं निशीथे
तामुन्निद्रामवनिशयनां सौधवातायनस्थः ॥ ८५ ॥

आधिक्षामां विरहशयने संनिषण्णैकपार्श्वां
प्राचीमूले तनुमिव कलामात्रशेषां हिमांशोः ।
नीता रात्रिः क्षण इव मया सार्धमिच्छारतैर्या
तामेवोष्णैर्विरहमहतीमश्रुभिर्यापयन्तीम् ॥ ८६ ॥

निःश्वासेनाधरकिसलयक्लेशिना विक्षिपन्तीं
शुद्धस्नानात्परुषमलकं नूनमागण्डलम्बम् ।
मत्संभोगः कथमुपनमेत्स्वप्नजोऽपीति निद्रा-
माकाङ्क्षन्तीं नयनसलिलोत्पीडरुद्धावकाशम् ॥ ८७ ॥

85

Your friend, I fear, suffers separation more
in the night with nothing to do than in the day
with its diversions. So you must then, standing
at midnight by the window of our house, see
that faithful girl—sleepless, her bed the floor—
to console her fully with my message.

86

Wasted by sadness, sunk on one side of the bed
of separation like the moon's figure shrunk
to its least crescent in the eastern sky, she's forced
to get through a night stretched by absence, her tears
scalding, the same night that passed like an instant
when I was there pleasing her in every wish.

87

Surely sighing as she parches her lower lip
like a new shoot, blowing aside the hair
hanging at her cheeks and left harsh by rinses
of mere water, she thinks, while she longs for sleep,
how we yet could hold each other, if only in dreams,
but that sleep's passage is clogged by a flood of tears.

आद्ये बद्धा विरहदिवसे या शिखा दाम हित्वा
	शापस्यान्ते विगलितशुचा तां मयोद्द्रेष्टनीयाम् ।
स्पर्शक्लिष्टामयमितनखेनासकृत्सारयन्तीं
	गण्डाभोगात्कठिनविषममामेकवेणीं करेण ॥ ८८ ॥

पादानिन्दोरमृतशिशिराञ्जालमार्गप्रविष्टा-
	न्पूर्वप्रीत्या गतमभिमुखं संनिवृत्तं तथैव ।
चक्षु: खेदात्सलिलगुरुभि: पक्ष्मभिश्छादयन्तीं
	साभ्रेऽह्नीव स्थलकमलिनीं नप्रबुद्धां नसुप्तान् ॥ ८९ ॥

सा संन्यस्ताभरणमबला पेशलं धारयन्ती
	शय्योत्सङ्गे निहितमसकृद्दुःखदुःखेन गात्रम् ।
त्वामप्यस्रं नवजलमयं मोचयिष्यत्यवश्यं
	प्राय: सर्वो भवति करुणावृत्तिरार्द्रान्तरात्मा ॥ ९० ॥

88

That stiff and scratchy braid that she brushes again
and again from her round cheek with a hand
whose nails she's neglected to trim—that very braid
was plaited from her hair, its garland flung off, the day
of our parting, to be unwoven by me,
released from sorrow at the end of the curse.

89

Tears of grief weighting the lashes
she would cover her eyes with, those eyes—meeting
the moonlight, a joy to her once, that comes through
the lattice window, cooled with nectar—
will turn quickly aside like the land-lotus
on a cloudy day, not fully opened or closed.

90

She, unsteady, supporting with terrible pain
her body, ornaments laid by,
sinking down to our bed again
and again, will surely cause you to shed
new water for tears, for it's true
that the melted heart is prone to pity.

जाने सख्यास्तव मयि मनः संभृतस्नेहमस्मा-
  दित्थंभूता प्रथमविरहे तामहं तर्कयामि ।
वाचालं मां न खलु सुभगंमन्यभावः करोति
  प्रत्यक्षं ते निखिलमचिराद्भ्रातरुक्तं मया यत् ॥ ८१ ॥

रुद्धापाङ्गप्रसरमलकैरञ्जनस्नेहशून्यं
  प्रत्यादेशादपि च मधुनो विस्मृतभ्रूविलासम् ।
त्वय्यासन्ने नयनमुपरिस्पन्दि शङ्के मृगाक्ष्या
  मीनक्षोभाच्चलकुवलयश्रीतुलामेष्यतीति ॥ ८२ ॥

वामश्चास्याः कररुहपदैर्मुच्यमानो मदीयै-
  र्मुक्ताजालं चिरपरिचितं त्याजितो दैवगत्या ।
संभोगान्ते मम समुचितो हस्तसंवाहनानां
  यास्यत्यूरुः सरसकदलीस्तम्भगौरश्चलत्वम् ॥ ८३ ॥

91

I know that your friend's heart is laden with love
for me, so I fancy her brought to such a state
because of this, our first parting.
It's not vanity that makes me seem
immoderate. What I've said, brother,
you'll soon have wholly before your eyes.

92

Dry without its collyrium, its side-
long glance partially blocked by hair, forgetting
how to play because she abstains from wine, the eye
of that fawnlike girl, I think, will feel its lid
throb when you come near, and will match the beauty
of the blue lotus fluttered by the stir of fish.

93

And her left thigh—lacking the marks
of my nails, deprived by hostile fate
of the old familiar web of pearls,
so used to my kneading hand
after we'd loved, and pale as a plantain's
moist stem—will start to throb.

तस्मिन्काले जलद यदि सा लब्धनिद्रासुखा स्या-
        दन्वास्यैनां स्तनितविमुखो याममात्रं सहस्व ।
मा भूदस्याः प्रणयिनि मयि स्वप्नलब्धे कथंचि-
        त्सद्यःकण्ठच्युतभुजलताग्रन्थि गाढोपगूढम् ।। ६४ ।।

तामुत्थाप्य स्वजलकणिकाशीतलेनानिलेन
        प्रत्याश्वस्तां सममभिनवैर्जालकैर्मालतीनाम् ।
विद्युद्गर्भः स्तिमितनयनां त्वत्सनाथे गवाक्षे
        वक्तुं धीरः स्तनितवचनैर्मानिनीं प्रक्रमेथाः ।। ६५ ।।

भर्तुर्मित्रं प्रियमविधवे विद्धि मामाम्बुवाहं
        तत्संदेशैर्हृदयनिहितैरागतं त्वत्समीपम् ।
यो वृन्दानि त्वरयति पथि श्राम्यतां प्रोषितानां
        मन्द्रस्निग्धैर्ध्वनिभिरबलावेणिमोक्षोत्सुकानि ।। ६६ ।।

94

If then, O Cloud, she should have the pleasure of sleep,
you must wait for one watch of the night,
sitting behind her, stifling your thunder,
so that when she has somehow found me—her dearest—
in a dream of loving, our arms, involved as vines,
won't suddenly fall away from their hold.

95

Waking her with a breeze cooled
by your dew when she is freshened along
with the buds of the mālatī, you should begin—
your lightning withheld—to speak gravely
in words of thunder to the proud girl
whose eyes are fixed on the window you fill.

96

'Know me, woman whose mate still lives,
as a dear friend of your lord, a cloud come to you
with his message deep in my heart,
I who urge on their way with soft
plangent sounds crowds of tired travellers
longing to loosen the braids of their wives.'

इत्याख्याते पवनतनयं मैथिलावोन्मुखी सा
	त्वामुत्कण्ठोच्छ्वसितहृदया वीक्ष्य संभाव्य चैव ।
श्रोष्यत्यस्मात्परमवहिता सौम्य सीमन्तिनीनां
	कान्तोदन्तः सुहृदुपनतः संगमात्किंचिदूनः ॥ ८७ ॥

तामायुष्मन्मम च वचनादात्मनश्चोपकर्तुं
	ब्रूया एवं तव सहचरो रामगिर्याश्रमस्थः ।
अव्यापन्नः कुशलमबले पृच्छति त्वां वियुक्तः
	पूर्वाभाष्यं सुलभविपदां प्राणिनामेतदेव ॥ ८८ ॥

अङ्गेनाङ्गं प्रतनु तनुना गाढतप्तेन तप्तं
	साश्रेणाश्रुद्रुतमविरतोत्कण्ठमुत्कण्ठितेन ।
उष्णोच्छ्वासं समधिकतरोच्छ्वासिना दूरवर्ती
	संकल्पैस्तैर्विशति विधिना वैरिणा रुद्धमार्गः ॥ ८९ ॥

This said, her heart lifting
with desire, her face upturned like Sītā's
to Hanumān as she sees and greets you, she'll listen
closely after that. News of their lovers
brought by a friend, O Gentle One, is only
less than real reunion to women.

Because, My Lord, I've asked you and to honor yourself,
you should say this to her: 'Your mate, staying
at a retreat on Rāmagiri and still alive,
wonders how you are in his absence, lady'—
this surely is the first question to ask
the living who so easily come to grief.

'He, far off, a hostile fate blocking
his way, by mere wish joins his body
with your body, his thinness with your thinness,
his pain with your intense pain, his tears
with your tears, his endless longing
with your longing, his deep sigh with your sigh.

शब्दाख्येयं यदपि किल ते यः सखीनां पुरस्ता-
    त्कर्णे लोकः कथयितुमभूदाननस्पर्शलोभात् ।
सोऽतिक्रान्तः श्रवणविषयं लोचनाभ्यामदृष्ट-
    स्त्वामुत्कण्ठाविरचितपदं मन्मुखेनेदमाह ॥ १०० ॥

श्यामास्वङ्गं चकितहरिणीप्रेक्षणे दृष्टिपातं
    वक्त्रच्छायां शशिनि शिखिनां बर्हभारेषु केशान् ।
उत्पश्यामि प्रतनुषु नदीवीचिषु भ्रूविलासान्
    हन्तैकस्मिन्क्वचिदपि न ते चण्डि सादृश्यमस्ति ॥ १०१ ॥

त्वामालिख्य प्रणयकुपितां धातुरागैः शिलाया-
    मात्मानं ते चरणपतितं यावदिच्छामि कर्तुम् ।
अस्रैस्तावन्मुहुरुपचितैर्दृष्टिरालुप्यते मे
    क्रूरस्तस्मिन्नपि न सहते संगमं नौ कृतान्तः ॥ १०२ ॥

82

100

He, who just because he wanted to touch
your face was once so quick to whisper
what easily could have been said aloud
among women companions, but now too far for ears
to hear or eyes to see, speaks through my mouth
these words that his passion composed.

101

"In the shyāma vines I see your limbs, your look
in the eye of a startled doe, the loveliness
of your face in the moon, in the peacock's plumage your hair,
the playful lift of your brows in the light ripples
of rivers, but, O, sadly, nowhere, my passionate girl,
is the whole of your likeness in any one of these.

102

With red rock I've drawn you on a stone slab,
feigning anger, but however much I want
to portray myself fallen there at your feet,
my eyes are clouded with tears that
well up over and over. So hard is this fate
that won't permit even our pictured union.

मामाकाशप्रणिहितभुजं निर्दयाश्लेषहेतो-
  र्लब्धायास्ते कथमपि मया स्वप्नसंदर्शनेषु ।
पश्यन्तीनां न खलु बहुशो न स्थलीदेवतानां
  मुक्तास्थूलास्तरुकिसलयेष्वश्रुलेशाः पतन्ति ॥ १०३ ॥

भित्वा सद्यः किसलयपुटान्देवदारुद्रुमाणां
  ये तत्क्षीरस्रुतिसुरभयो दक्षिणेन प्रवृत्ताः ।
आलिङ्ग्यन्ते गुणवति मया ते तुषाराद्रिवाताः
  पूर्वं स्पृष्टं यदि किल भवेदङ्गमेभिस्तवेति ॥ १०४ ॥

संक्षिप्येत क्षण इव कथं दीर्घयामा त्रियामा
  सर्वावस्थास्वहरपि कथं मन्दमन्दातपं स्यात् ।
इत्थं चेतश्चटुलनयने दुर्लभप्रार्थनं मे
  गाढोष्माभिः कृतमशरणं त्वद्वियोगव्यथाभिः ॥ १०५ ॥

103

The goddesses of this region shed
tears as big as pearls on the branches
of trees because they see me here,
my arms stretched out to empty air
because I want fiercely to clutch you,
somehow found in the vision of dreams.

104

O my perfect one, those winds
off the Himālayas that suddenly open
the budding deodar shoots and now blow
southward scented with the ooze of their resin,
I hug close to myself, thinking
maybe they have touched your body.

105

Is there some way the long watches
of night could shrink to an instant, and the day
be made always temporate?
Thus, my heart, wanting what can't be had—
you, with the shy glance—is left helpless
by pain from the wasting fire of absence.

नन्वात्मानं बहु विगणयन्नात्मनैवावलम्बे
	तत्कल्याणि त्वमपि नितरां मा गमः कातरत्वम् ।
कस्यात्यन्तं सुखमुपनतं दुःखमेकान्ततो वा
	नीचैर्गच्छत्युपरि च दशा चक्रनेमिक्रमेण ॥ १०६ ॥

शापान्तो मे भुजगशयनादुत्थिते शार्ङ्गपाणौ
	शेषान्मासान्गमय चतुरो लोचने मीलयित्वा ।
पश्चादावां विरहगुणितं तं तमात्माभिलाषं
	निर्वेक्ष्यावः परिणतशरच्चन्द्रिकासु क्षपासु ॥ १०७ ॥

भूयश्चाह त्वमपि शयने कण्ठलग्ना पुरा मे
	निद्रां गत्वा किमपि रुदती सस्वरं विप्रबुद्धा ।
सान्तर्हासं कथितमसकृत्पृछतश्च त्वया मे
	दृष्टः स्वप्ने कितव रमयन्कामपि त्वं मयेति ॥ १०८ ॥

106

And so, musing much to myself,
I keep myself alive, and you,
my dear, must not give way to grief.
Whose life is all pleasure
or always pain? Luck goes under
and up like the rim of a rolling wheel.

107

When Vishṇu has risen from his serpent bed
my curse is done. Shutting your eyes,
make the last four months pass by.
Then we'll unleash under the bright moon
of autumn nights all the desires
held back while we were far apart."

108

And tell her I said this: "Once
in bed, though clinging in sleep to my neck,
for some reason you woke crying aloud,
and when I asked why again and again, answered
with an inward smile: *You cheat, I saw you
playing with another woman in my sleep!*

एतस्मान्मां कुशलिनमभिज्ञानदानाद्विदित्वा
    मा कौलीनादसितनयने मय्यविश्वासिनी भू: ।
स्नेहानाहु: किमपि विरहे ध्वंसिनस्ते त्वभोगा-
    दिष्टे वस्तुन्युपचितरसा: प्रेमराशीभवन्ति ॥ १०९ ॥

कच्चित्सौम्य व्यवसितमिदं बन्धुकृत्यं त्वया मे
    प्रत्यादेशान्न खलु भवतो धीरतां कल्पयामि ।
नि:शब्दोऽपि प्रदिशसि जलं याचितश्चातकेभ्य:
    प्रत्युक्तं हि प्रणयिषु सतामीप्सितार्थक्रियैव ॥ ११० ॥

एतत्कृत्वा प्रियमनुचितप्रार्थनावर्तिनो मे
    सौहार्दाद्वा विधुर इति वा मय्यनुक्रोशबुद्ध्या ।
इष्टान्देशाञ्जलद विचर प्रावृषा संभृतश्री-
    र्मा भूदेवं क्षणमपि च ते विद्युता विप्रयोग: ॥ १११ ।

109

Knowing by these signs that I'm well, O don't,
my dark-eyed girl, let lies make you doubt me.
People say—who can tell why?—
that absence withers passion from lack
of pleasure. But desires, made all the keener
for what they crave, swell into love."

110

I trust, friend, that you'll do this for me
and am certain your grave look does not
forebode refusal. You silently grant
the chātakas the rain they crave.
For the answer of good men to those
who ask their help is simply to do what's desired.

111

Having done this favor for me (who asked more
than I should have asked), whether from friendship or compassion
for my lonely state, now wander, Cloud,
wherever you will, your glory swelled by rain.
And may you never—even for an instant—be
parted like me, from your lightning."

Appendix I
Commentary

General Remarks

The *Meghadūta* has traditionally been divided into two parts, *pūrvamegha* (early) and *uttaramegha* (latter); these are apparently meant to distinguish the stanzas covering the cloud's imagined journey from those covering its arrival at the Yaksha's home, Alakā. But this particular division (between stanzas 63 and 64 in my version) is open to some doubt and has not always been observed, even in some early commentaries.[1] There are, in fact, more than two parts to the *Meghadūta*, especially if one wishes to mark those points at which the poem changes the scope of its concerns. For example, stanzas 1 to 12 constitute a preamble; 13 serves as transition to a much longer section up to 63, which describes the cloud's journey northward. Stanza 63 is again transitional, leading to a description of Alakā, concluded at 71. Here attention narrows to a description of the Yaksha's own residence to 77, another transition which again narrows the focus, this time to the Yaksha's mate. This section continues to 93, which

---

[1] See S. K. De, *The Megha-Dūta of Kālidāsa* (New Delhi, 1957), p. 59.

91

together with 94 constitutes a transition to the delivery of the message, which itself extends from 96 through 109. The final two stanzas of the poem close the address to the cloud. These divisions should, of course, be noted, but they do not constitute major breaks in the plot or movement of the poem. Rather they indicate continual narrowing of attention to the climactic meeting of the cloud and the Yaksha's mate. It seems to me sufficient to observe this narrowing without overemphasizing transitions in the poem.

There are several others matters that have concerned editors and other translators of the *Meghadūta* which I may seem to have slighted, and no doubt an explanation is in order. First, I include no road map from Rāmagiri to Alakā; from my introduction, it must be clear that I regard the ideal landscape to be the main matter of audience concern. Therefore, the map drawn by the Yaksha's imagination is the only one necessary to an understanding of the poem. Second, I have avoided speculating on the precise nature of the dereliction in duty that brought about the Yaksha's exile. The text provides no basis for such speculation, and the matter, given the actual concerns of the poem, is of no importance. Besides, to look for motives in the Yaksha's life outside the poem is to confuse literature with life, and possibly to mislead readers into judging works on how well they ape common reality, a view that would have appalled Sanskrit poets and renders the whole of Sanskrit poetry prima facie worthless.

Another convention I have eschewed in the commentary below is that of glossing names merely for the sake of glossing, though at the end of this section I have added a Finding List of the less familiar terms for quick reference. Affixing Latin or Greek appellations to flowers seems to me to involve the same confusion of art with life as hunting up the pre-poem biography of literary characters. Even if Kālidāsa was careful to place his plants in the right place at the right season, he was less concerned with their literal counterparts than with exploiting the richness of sound and of allusion summoned up by their names. Milton's flower catalogue in "Lycidas" and Keats' floral allusions in "Ode to a Nightingale" have much the same purpose.

Finally, the reader will notice that I never allude to the Yaksha's mate as his wife or spouse, though other translators do so. I avoid these terms mainly because they resonate a side of domesticity—certainly to Western ears—that never appears in the *Meghadūta*. What we do see there is a relationship between the ideal courtly lover and his ideal lady, the *Nāyaka* and *Nāyikā* of Sanskrit literary tradition. There is no reason to regard their love as less serious than those solemnized by orthodox ritual. Indeed, a traditional Indian name for union without benefit of clergy is the Gāndharva marriage. Gandharvas are, like Yakshas, demigods. The term Gāndharva marriage, then, suggests the way in which it was imagined all such creatures became mates—through mutual consent based on mutual desire.

Detailed Analysis

Stanzas 1–13: This unit establishes reader expectation by setting the pervasive tone, the time, place, and character, though the poet expends little effort on the last; so unconcerned is Kālidāsa with the Yaksha's psychology that, with only the slightest bow to plausibility, he explains his protagonist's irrational behavior as the result of love-sickness reinforced by the presence of the awesome sign of the rainy season itself.

The Yaksha's actual address to the cloud takes the form of a traditional supplication, mixing the pathos of the supplicant's condition with flattery for his benefactor along with the promise of reward for performing what is asked. Contained in the supplication is a brief synopsis of the journey which will be elaborated in the body of the poem; such foretelling is a convention of Indian poetry, effective because Indian audiences did not expect novel facts or the resolution of suspense in their poetry. Instead, they expected to find what they already knew, rendered in some especially beautiful and unique way. So the foretelling serves to whet audience appetite, perhaps in the manner of a sleight-of-hand expert who tells what he is going to perform and even sometimes how he is going to perform it, and then astonishes everyone by making the performance still appear to be magic.

Throughout the synopsis and in the request in 12 that the cloud begin its mission, Kālidāsa also establishes a motif that will persist and grow throughout the poem; that is, the strong sense of relationship among all parts of the world, with the cloud at the center, either stimulating union or bringing to mind comparisons suggesting it. Thus, the audience is immediately reminded of the ties of sentiment aroused by the cloud's presence as a sign of rain, of the kinship of cloud and birds, and of the affection between mountain and cloud. These are oblique statements of that underlying unity of things which supports the celebratory tone of the poem, and they are made with a fine irony that the Sanskrit audience would have appreciated; for it is the Yaksha's very sense of separation that makes him perceive—on the verge of the season of union—the abiding and joyously intimate connection of all things in nature.

Stanzas 14–63: Though this section constitutes a single entity—a catalogue of locales the cloud will see on its journey north—it, in fact, is divisible into smaller units, themselves pervaded by the general pattern of the cloud's activities. This pattern consists of repeated drinking from the rivers it passes over, followed by resting on the slopes of the mountain peaks it comes to. In the Yaksha's erotic imaginings, the drinking from various rivers is equated with sexual intercourse.

Earlier in the poem, the extraordinary nature of the cloud has been touched upon: its massiveness (2), nobility (6), generosity (7), efficaciousness (11), and affectionateness (12). These traits are amplified and extended in this second section until something like supernatural status is conferred on the cloud. For example, in 14, rising from the *nichulas* for its journey north, it is mistaken for a mountain top by the wives of the Siddhas, certain semi-divine beings noted for their purity. Their innocent wonder provides a way to measure the startling magnitude of the cloud. So, too, does the assertion at the end of the stanza that the divine elephants of the directions, who support the universe, consider it a worthy challenger of their strength. Indian myth associates elephants with clouds in a number of ways ranging from resemblance to actual kinship.[2] Kālidāsa exploits these associations throughout the poem.

In 15, the cloud's supernatural character is enhanced by the comparison to Vishnu; the selection of that deity's Krishna avatar for the comparison not only refers to the natural color of the water-laden cloud, but also suggests its erotic aspect. The lore concerning the rainbow is complex and perhaps not of primary importance to understanding the comparison itself; however, the fact that the term for rainbow in the original is "The Breaker's (Indra's) Bow" lends some magnitude to the cloud since Indra is king of heaven. Of lesser import is the significance of the anthill, either a proper name for a literal peak or, perhaps, as Kale suggests, an actual anthill, so that the rainbow would be explained, according to traditional lore, as the beams radiated up from the jeweled hood of a great serpent living in it.[3]

After the reminder in 16 of the cloud's intense relation to the fruitfulness of the land, the drinking-resting pattern begins in earnest, but is inset with vivid detail and with allusions to traditional lore, serving mostly the transformation of the landscape into some manifestation of love, summoned forth by the coming of the cloud.

Although mountains are usually perceived as male, in 18, Āmrakūṭa, covered with ripe mangos, is compared to a great breast. Mangos, here, also are meant to imply human fruition, just as most of the allusions to flora in the rest of the poem are meant to signify either human flowering or beauty. In some instances, as with the *kakubhas* whose fragrance tempts the cloud to stop on the peaks where it grows (22), flowers are perceived

[2] See H. Zimmer, *Myths and Symbols in Indian Art and Civilizations*, ed., Joseph Cambell (New York, 1946), pp. 102–109.

[3] See M. R. Kale, *The Meghadūta of Kālidāsa* (Bombay, n.d.), p. 33.

as a kind of offering of welcome suggesting either worship or affection.[4]

Animal allusions, also, have something like emblematic meaning, usually, though not always, with erotic overtones. In 20, for example, the Yaksha asserts that the Revā's waters will taste of the exudation of rutting elephants. Already we have seen that the elephant can serve as a measure for magnitude and force; now it functions to suggest overpowering sexuality.

In 21 the cloud's capacity to freshen the earth acts like a magnet, drawing creatures after it to enjoy the effects of its passing. Its power to transform nature into a complex of loving relations is extended to encompass even what might appear to be outside the range of legitimate sexuality: in 25, the cloud, if only by its presence, is associated with the "bought women" whose perfume fills the caves on Nīchais' slope.

The detail which enriches the drinking-resting pattern throughout all these stanzas is the human presence, particularly of beautiful women of all types—the prostitutes in 25, the flower harvesters in 26, the idle flirts at the court of Ujjayinī in 27. These references are nicely positioned between the cloud's amorous drinking in of rivers, so that the audience is never allowed long to forget the pervasive presence of female erotic intensity that grips the Yaksha's imagination. The human embodiments of that intensity are transposed to natural phenomena in the same way that the attributes of one element in a comparison get transferred to the other. Thus, what might have seemed a rather labored personification of the Nirvindhyā River in 28, is less arbitrary following the description of human seductiveness in the preceding stanzas.

Kālidāsa is careful to keep the erotic before us in even the most perfunctory allusions, as in the seemingly off-hand reference in 30 to "Udayana's story," which the old countrymen of Avantī know "by heart"; so too would his audience, for King Udayana was a popular hero whose love for the Princess Vāsavadattā

[4] See F. and E. Edgerton, *The Cloud Messenger* (Ann Arbor, 1964), p. 84.

provided plots for other writers in whose work the king is perceived as the model of the gallant courtly lover.

In the same stanza, the poet manages to link the erotic with the moral in his description of Vishālā (another name for Ujjayinī), comparing the city to a fragment of heaven brought down by those who, having exhausted their religious merit, have had to return to earth. This linking of what in the West might seem hardly compatible categories of action would not have troubled an Indian audience which saw no conflict among the three ideal earthly goals proposed by their culture: *dharma* (righteousness), *artha* (wealth), and *kāma* (pleasure). In fact, the upright man ought to expect as the reward for his virtue both wealth and pleasure. So it should be no surprise to find all three values drawn from in various combinations to enhance the wonder of some person, place, or thing.

Indeed, in the next few stanzas Kālidāsa moves us through descriptions of animal and human sexuality in an environment of great wealth to an elaborate treatment of Mahākāla, Ujjayinhrī's great shrine to Shiva, the "Master of the Three Worlds" and husband to the mother goddess, one of whose names is Chaṇḍī. And here a holy sanctuary is comfortably defined in terms of wealth and pleasure (particularly in 35) as well as by the piety associated with cloud's service to the god (34). Both Kālidāsa and his audience shared the very unwestern assumption that there is no separate sphere of religion isolated from the worldly. The sacred also participates in the complex of relations and correspondences that make up the ethos of the poem.

In this sequence (34–37), the cloud continues to serve in its usual roles: an almost divine mediator for union or harmony among the parts of the world, a great saving agent, and a release for pent-up desire. Thus, the cloud is associated with divinity by being mistaken for the darkness ringing Shiva's throat. According to Indian lore, the god acquired this hue when, in order to save the world, he swallowed the poison churned up from the Ocean of Milk: the great undifferentiated mass stirred by the gods in order to obtain from it *amrita*, the immortalizing nectar.

The cloud's association with divinity is further extended when it is invited to use its thunder to serve as Shiva's drum in the god's great ritual dance and to provide him a cloak in lieu of the blood-soaked hide of a demon-elephant slain by Shiva. The complex of allusions concerning the elephant hide is highly compressed. When the demon, Gaya, in elephant form, threatened to annihilate the sages, Shiva came to their aid by forcing Gaya to dance with him until Gaya collapsed. Shiva then ripped off his hide, threw it over his shoulders and performed his wild victory dance, the *Tāṇḍava*. In 36 of the *Meghadūta*, the god is apparently about to commemorate ritually that victory over evil, no less terrifying for its being a ritual repetition; this explains the fear in the eyes of his consort (here called Bhavānī).[5]

Amid all this awesome power and destruction, the cloud's power to soothe is measured by its calming effect on the great goddess as she watches her husband begin his terrible dance. The same comforting effect has already worked on the human level in 35, where the weary temple dancers are refreshed by the cloud's soothing rain.

In 37, the cloud, like Shiva himself, exhibits a double nature, both beneficent and frightening: its lightning can show the way to lovers' assignations, but its thunder can terrify. Nor would it have appeared confusing to the Sanskrit audience that the cloud's lightning should be seen as a means of illumination in this stanza and in the next be personified as the cloud's own mate. In a world of correspondences, the same element, seen in different contexts, would be expected to suggest different congruences.

The audience would note that once again the cloud has moved out of the divine and human into the natural world, ready to resume its journey. Yet not completely out, for the sun in 39 is personified as a competing lover, and once more we are reminded of the kinship and correspondence in a world imagined by love.

In the next few stanzas the general pattern resumes, with another interruption in 43 at the shrine of Skanda, the war

⁵ Zimmer, *op. cit.*, pp. 172–173.

god. The two allusions to religious sanctuaries in such close proximity are not merely the result of the literal fact that one follows close after the other on the cloud's itinerary. Kālidāsa could easily have passed over the latter with the barest mention. But his attentiveness to both indirectly alerts the audience to the fact that the cloud is nearing the most sacred precincts of India, the Himālyas, where divinity is as much at home as humans are in Ujjayinī. And since the poem celebrates its culture, Skanda's shrine, like Shiva's, is a fit place for reverent attention. But even here the sexual is also brought into play, suggesting, with other kinds of binding sentiment, connectedness. For the Yaksha alludes in an abbreviated form to the miraculous birth of Skanda, whose conception began with Shiva flinging his semen into the mouth of the fire god, Agni, who in turn deposited it in the Gangā, among whose reeds the deity was finally born. Still other conventional allusions establish a complex of loving relations: Skanda's cherished vehicle, the peacock, and Bhavānī's indulgent affection for her son. Though in 43, Skanda's birth is represented as occurring without the participation of a woman, Shiva's consort is often referred to as his mother, as is Gangā who received his seed from Agni's mouth. The strange inconsistencies in the explanation of Skanda's origins may derive from its being a composite of different myths concerning the god.[6]

Two more allusions complete this section: the reference to "pairs of Siddhas" with their lutes, mildly suggestive of the erotic, and the reference to Rantideva whose sacrifice of a multitude of cows caused the creation of the Charmanvatī River when the flowing blood of the slain animals was miraculously transformed into water. Here the lore of great piety is used in conjunction with the lore of erotic and familiar affection to establish correspondence and to show how Indian earth was—in the oldest sense of that word—cultivated, made usable and significant to men.

Resuming its pattern at 47, the cloud descends to drink

[6] See S. Bhattacharji, *The Indian Theogony: A Comparative Study of Indian Mythology from the Vedas to the Puranas* (Cambridge, England: 1970), pp. 182–183.

from the river created by Rantideva's sacrifice and in doing so, appears to have taken on the dark hue of Krishṇa, a reminder again of its semi-divine status. But more important, Kālidāsa demonstrates what can be done with idealizing distance, putting us at such a height that the union of cloud and water can be seen as an elegant artifact—a strand of pearls with a sapphire pendant. Nature, in this transformation, finds similitude in art created to adorn human beauty, and again—for those who have the eyes, *and the perspective, to see*—rich connections are revealed.

Kālidāsa's ability to bring everything into the complex of relations that make up the ethos of the poem is tested severely in 48, when the cloud crosses the field of the Kurus; this is the battleground on which, in the epic *Mahābhārata*, vast armies slaughtered each other, leaving only a few heroes alive. So massive is the lore suggested by this allusion to the great epic and so well-known to his audience, that, had the poet brought it too much forward, he could have upset the poise of the established tone, which is not heroic. In fact, the heroic here, embodied in the deeds of Arjuna, the greatest warrior in the epic, is kept in the background, serving merely as a comparison for the impact of the cloud's downpour on vulnerable lotus blossoms.

The allusion to Krishṇa's brother, Balarāma, in 49 also suggests the heroic; but again its force is subordinated to the pervasive sentiment of the poem. Balarāma, here seen as something of a pacifist and ascetic, refused to join the war between kinsmen that is the topic of the *Mahābhārata*. Instead, he spent his time purifying himself with the waters of the Sarasvatī, one of the most sacred rivers of the tradition, where the cloud is now about to refresh itself. Again, the connection between the super-human and the cloud is asserted; so too is the power of love in the brief mention of Revatī, Balarāma's wife.

When, in 50, the cloud reaches the Gaṅgā River (Jahnu's daughter), the allusions associated with this most sacred river are packed into a complex tour de force, merging the lore of piety, eroticism, and the iconography of Shiva in one of his representations—all to set forth the significance of the river.

However Kālidāsa's use of the epithet "Jahnu's daughter" for Gangā seems to be an instance of the poet's option, noted in the Introduction, to choose a synonym that fits his metrical need. For the epithet brings no significant effect to the poem. Lore has it that the flow of the Gangā interfered with the worship of a certain royal sage, Jahnu, who eliminated the nuisance by drinking up the river, but was later prevailed upon by gods and sages to release its waters. In this sense only is Gangā his daughter. But other allusions do function to define the river. For example, its power to purify is "demonstrated" in the mention of Sagara's sons, sixty thousand of whom were incinerated for disturbing the meditations of the sage, Kapila. Through acts of great piety, the Gangā was brought down from heaven so its waters, purifying the ashes of the victims, would permit them to rise to heaven. The river's other aspect, its divine charm, is characterized by its connection with Shiva who, according to lore, caught its waters in his great mat of hair as they fell from heaven. This story is transmuted into a domestic triangle, for Gangā is personified as the god's second wife and competitor with his first—the great goddess (here, Gaurī) who is jealous at Gangā's playful touseling of Shiva's mooncrowned hair; and Kālidāsa exploits the literary convention that laughter is white to represent Gangā's foam as a provocation to Gaurī.

The explanation is complex, but the actual unfolding would not have been so for a knowledgeable audience deeply engaged, if for no other reason, to see how the poet brings the rich fragments of lore into relation with each other and with the sentiment of the poem. They would remain engaged for the same reason by 51, in which, once again, the cloud is compared to a divine elephant. But the climax of this small section comes at the close of the stanza, where the union of cloud and river, dark and light, is made to appear (again in distant but astonished eyes) like the holiest confluence of rivers in India, that of the Yamunā and the Gangā. Here again, nature is transformed, this time by a combination of the erotic and sacred; beauty and goodness define the landscape, seen here in a union of purifying waters. The cloud serves, in this instance, as a reminder of that relationship.

It is no accident that the poem becomes denser with lore as it reaches the Himālayas, since this is divine territory and the proper home for great wonders, the "marvels" alluded to in 57. On these heights, which fathered the Gangā, the cloud rests (52), its hue compared to that of the earth pawed by Shiva's bull vehicle, Nandī, another reminder of the cloud's status; just as its virtues are suggested in the following verses: its beneficence in 53 and its wise force in 54, exhibited in its treatment of the fabulous *sharabhas*, beasts resembling deer, but possessing eight legs and undeerlike aggressiveness.

In 55, the cloud's piety is called into play by the holiness of the place where Shiva has left his footprint. This section attains a climax in the concert in which all things, natural and supernatural, join to hymn Shiva's destruction of the city of Tripura, once the home of the demons. The Kinnaras of 56 are another type of demigod whose special genius is for music. The cloud is again invited, as in 34, to fill the role of the drum with its thunder.

The general pattern of drinking and resting reaches its last phase at 57 as the cloud nears the Yaksha's city; but this last phase, though not the climax of the *Meghadūta*, achieves its own crescendo, for the landscape is more massively dramatic as its lifts toward the peaks of the mountains. Consequently the actions of the cloud seem more momentous. Both references at the end of 57 are heroic; the first, to "Bhrigu's lord," alludes to the mighty brahman fighter, Rāma of the Axe, who single-handedly slew the whole warrior caste and split Mount Krauncha with his arrows to make a passage-way through. The second, to Vishṇu, refers to that deity's victory over the demon, Bali, who had promised Vishṇu, in his dwarf avatar, as much territory as he could cover in three strides. With the first two, the god, taking his full form, covered heaven and earth; with his third, according to a common version of the myth, he reached beyond the vision of man. Here again, but on a gigantic scale, lore infuses landscape with meaning, and again the cloud is associated with divinity by its comparison to the god's huge impending foot.

In 58, the cloud attains the sacred summit of Kailāsa, the locus of Alakā, and the mountain's glacial brilliance and amplitude are foregrounded. This is partly accomplished by the allusion to the stupendous attempt of Rāvana, a mighty demon king, to steal the peak; he had such power that only Vishnu in his avatar as Rāma could destroy him, a feat that constitutes the climax of the *Rāmāyana*. Though he can change his shape, Rāvana is pictured typically as a huge terrifying figure with ten heads and twenty arms. Among the Rākshasas (demons of the most malefic kind), he was the wickedest, yet his ascetic feats gave him near invulnerability. His lawless audacity is embodied in the legend of his attempt to remove the sacred peak to his own capital in Lankā.

In the next stanza, the cloud takes its last rest before Alakā and is seen brilliantly dark against the snow, a contrast which is built into the epic comparison that follows in which the white mountain with the cloud resting on its slope is perceived as the heroic Balarāma in his black mantle—a sight that "will draw to itself steady-eyed looks," that is, gazes of entranced astonishment that serve to measure the scope of this marvel. Magnitude is heaped on magnitude in the next stanzas in which the cloud is asked to transform itself into a grand stairway of ice so that Gaurī, helped by Shiva, can stroll Kailāsa, their "pleasure mount."

Interrupted a moment by the erotic play of the bathers of 61, the cloud will take its last drink in Lake Mānasa (62) whose holy waters in the most sacred of places serve as a fitting climax to all the early drinking and resting. There, before its final task is undertaken, the cloud is given a little breather (in which it serves as a shade for Airāvata, Indra's elephant mount), toys with the garments hanging on the divine tree that grants all wishes, and plays with its shadow on the icy slopes.

In 63, it comes to the heavenly city of Alakā, and here its function changes; it will no longer be seen as the center of the action. Already, in this stanza, though the beginning of the *uttaramegha* is traditionally said to be at 64, the focus narrows to one object, the city. And it is no surprise that the first characteri-

103

zation of Alakā is erotic: it is the home of divine pleasure and it houses the object of the Yaksha's longing. In our first view of it, it is likened to a woman engaged in love-play; its cloud-topped mansions are compared to the head of a beautiful woman, a comparison in which its name, which can mean "curls", is exploited in a pun. Sanskrit literature treats this figure of speech far more seriously than ours, primarily because the phenomenon of double meaning is not regarded as an accident of language as it is with us, but as one more sign of the deeper correspondence of things.

Stanzas 64–71: The shift of focus to Alakā is accomplished in 64, which begins a long hyperbolic catalogue of the city's wonders. Here also the new role of the cloud is established; for instead of other material supplying comparisons to magnify the cloud, its qualities are now appropriated to heighten the value of Alakā, whose virtues are extolled through 71. These virtues are presented, typically, in terms of the abundance of Alakā's wealth and potential for pleasure, but also in terms of its power to transcend natural limits, as in the flower catalogue of 65 which, as the Edgertons point out, includes blossoms from each of the six Indian seasons, but all blooming simultaneously in Alakā.[7]

Though no longer at the center of things, the cloud's presence is still felt, for example, in the comparison of its thunder with the drums in 66, and more complexly, in the allusion in 67 to its role in releasing the moon's rays so that these in turn can release the soothing drops from moonstones—which are treated in lore as solidified moonlight—another suggestion of correspondence in the context of the erotic. This section culminates with the reference to the enmity between Shiva and the God of Love, Kāma. Since Shiva dwells in Alakā, the city is avoided by Kāma, who once was burned to ashes for having disturbed Shiva's meditations with his arrows. These arrows were tipped with flowers and shot from a bow whose string consisted of bees; thus the conceit in 71, comparing the glances of Alakā's divine girls to the love god's darts.

[7] Edgerton, *op. cit.*, p. 86.

Stanzas 72–78: At 72 the attention of the poem narrows again, this time to an intense and climactic focus on the Yaksha's own dwelling. Here the tone begins to modulate slowly from hyperbolic praise to the pathos befitting a description of love in separation. The note of pathos is struck immediately in the comparison of a "young Mandāra tree" to his mate's "proxy son," again with a suggestion of correspondence, here between nature and the human. But pathos is mixed with celebration in the loving attention that the Yaksha gives to the description of his residence in the next stanzas.

The cloud, though still peripheral to the Yaksha's attention, in 74 also makes its presence felt as a force for union; for its appearance reminds the speaker of the pleasure hill on the grounds of his home, his beloved's favorite spot. Traditional lore serves also in the next stanza to suggest correspondence and relationship, as in the personification of the ashoka and the amaranth trees which require, according to tradition, stimulation from a young woman in order to bloom. The trees, that is, experience the appetite of a pregnant woman for the strange and exotic. Lore has the ashoka requiring a woman's kick in order to blossom, the amaranth to be splashed with wine from a woman's mouth.[8] The Yaksha's description of his residence concludes in 77 with an allusion to a painting on its gates of the conch and lotus, both auspicious emblems either in their own forms or personified. But the concluding comparison of the house itself to a faded lotus gently mocks the efficacy of these charms.

Stanza 78 is transitional, leading to the most intense focus of the poem, the Yaksha's forlorn mate. In this stanza there is one more comparison of the cloud with the elephant, a last reminder of a major motif of the poem—the cloud's power, now adjusted to a benevolent diminution to accord with the character of its task.

Stanzas 79–95: The description of the Yaksha's beloved is based on a series of conventions as predictable in this circumstance as they are hyperbolic. The challenge to the poet is what he can

[8] Kale, *op. cit.*, pp. 132–133.

do with them by way of rich and elegant combinations. The conventions are simply a set of common formulae for treating woman's physical beauty, her character and feelings, and the effects on all these of separation from her lover. Western poetry during its medieval phase developed something like the same conventions, in which the term *affictio* referred to the prescribed head-to-toe description of a woman's physical attributes, and the term *notatio* to its counterpart in regard to her moral qualities. Sanskrit poets seem not so systematic as their Western counterparts in the use of this kind of convention. Kālidāsa distributes the formulaic materials with different degrees of elaboration through several stanzas. But the opening description of the woman's beauty in 79 is routinely straightforward, with the usual comparisons and hyperboles; her lower lip is likened to the bimba fruit (red), her eyes to those of a deer, her hips so full that her walking is slowed, her breasts so heavy as to cause her to stoop slightly—this capped by the hyperbolic compliment of the last line. This all serves the function of background for what follows: the detailed and pathetic description of what separation has done to her normal beauty, introduced in 80 with the allusion to the *chakravākī* bird, fated always to be apart from its mate at night and consequently signifying the lamenting lover in separation.

The next stanzas more directly show the effects of separation on the Yaksha's mate; they do so somewhat in the way Keats establishes pathos in "To Autumn," that is, by stylized portraits of a woman in one or another solitary and melancholy pose. In the *Meghadūta*, the personification is not of a season, but of a woman suffering in her lover's absence, so the pathos is more specific and intense. But the portraits are almost as allegorical, usually signifying distracted grief. Thus we see in 81 her tearful face cupped in her hands, her hair dishevelled; in 82 she is seen in the act of devotion, or sketching her far-off beloved, or conversing with the *sarikā*—here, a sad reminder of loving relation. In 83, she is posed, lute on her lap, its strings dampened by tears, a reference which should call to mind the mention in 45 of the

106

Siddha pairs who avoid the cloud's path so that their lutes will not suffer the same fate. The contrast here is between love in union and love in separation. Finally, in 84, she is pictured counting with blossoms the remaining days of separation or lost in erotic revery.

Despite its lesser role at this point, the cloud is not permitted to fade too far into the background, for in 81 it serves as comparative material to enhance the pathetic description. The pathos intensifies beginning in 85 when the cloud's "friend" (a polite epithet for the Yaksha's mate indicating no intimacy) is shown passing the night when torments of separation are at their worst. The pathos is underscored by contrasts with past pleasures as in 89. Stanza 91 could, however, seem to break the tone, but in fact aims to reinforce it by the predicted testimony of the cloud's behavior when it will see her; then, according to the Yaksha, in a handsome conceit, the cloud will be forced to weep. In this stanza, too, the intensity of his mate's suffering is explained as the result of the depth of her love and of this being their first separation. Though Kālidāsa is little concerned with psychological verisimilitude here (or anywhere else), he must remove what might be regarded as the narrator's vanity in his confidence that his mate is pining for him.

Stanza 92 resumes the direct portrait of sorrow, but with a hint of the union to come by the allusion to the throbbing lid, a sign of impending good, as is, in 93, the throbbing of the left thigh. But the erotic also enters the portrait in this stanza with the mention of conventional signs of passionate love-making, nail marks, here noticeable for their absence on the flesh of the Yaksha's mate. Also the cloud here resumes its earlier role of universal matchmaker, this time as a herald of good news looking toward eventual union of the lovers. Stanzas 94 and 95 serve as transition and preamble to the imagined delivery of the message.

Stanzas 96–109: In 96, the cloud introduces itself and states its mission. It is careful (in the Yaksha's imagination) to assert first its connection with her beloved and the fact that the latter still lives; only when these most urgent matters are dispensed with can it state its purpose and characterize itself as the ally of those suffering in separation. In 97, the Yaksha imagines his mate's response by drawing from the epic background of the *Rāmāyaṇa*: that moment in the story when Sītā, abducted by Rāvaṇa, sees Rāma's messenger, Hanumān.[9] Again Kālidāsa subdues epic lore to less heroic purposes to express only the intense joy in the event, a sentiment explained by the generalization that concludes the stanza.

This kind of generalizing, it should be noted, is frequently found in the poem, as a sort of pause or break in narration. It functions as an aside, often to the audience outside the poem (though often ostensibly directed to some audience inside it). It is a tool of traditional poetry, both in India and the West, although contemporary poets shy away from it as unpoetic, perhaps because it is a rhetorical device that draws its authority from a large pool of generalized common lore—almost dried up in our day. It has traditionally served, along with folk adages, to explain or justify individual behavior, appearance, or what have you, in terms of larger normative categories. Often it justifies or explains what might seem odd, implausible, or exceptional. This is how it functions when Homer has the desperate Odysseus pray to the deity of a certain stream: "Even the immortal gods do not rebuff a poor wanderer who comes to them for help."[10] In 97 of the *Meghadūta*, the technique makes plausible what might seem a somewhat overeager reaction to the cloud's first words.

The message itself begins at 98, first pressing home simple but urgent details. But this is a mere preamble to the masterful tour de force of the next stanza, which English can only produce a shadow of, since it lacks the means of the original language. Because it can link nouns and adjectives by inflection, Sanskrit permits Kālidāsa to unite the lovers through a series of paired words that transform, at its most painful moment, love in separation into a union of suffering.[11] And this union is so intense that

[9] See above, p. 24 n. 9.

[10] *The Odyssey*, Homer, trans, E. V. Rieu (Harmondsworth, 1946), p. 99.

[11] The words are, so to speak, fused by their being identical or nearly identical in form and joined by the inflected ending, the effect supplemented by the modi-

all the earlier ones, overseen or experienced by the cloud, seem mere facile foreplay.

Stanza 99, in fact, is the tonal climax of the poem, though what follows it is not quite anticlimax; for here the Yaksha describes the effects of separation on his own life, and they too have been devastating. In 100, for example, his anguish is rendered by a contrast between past happy states and the present; in 101, by his seeing her beauty piecemeal in one aspect of nature or another, but never finding in nature her whole beauty. In 102, he describes his futile attempts to sketch himself and his beloved together, failing because tears cloud his eyes; in 103, he asserts that his pain has even moved the local goddesses to tears. In 104 he recounts, most movingly, how he hugs to himself winds coming from the north because they may have touched her body; and in 105 he confesses his helplessness in the face of separation. Throughout this long plaint, the motif of correspondences established early in the poem serves as a background, found most obviously in the resemblances between human and natural beauty and in the sense of connectedness implied in imagining the wind as a link between lovers, a role the cloud has largely played before and, as messenger, still plays. So the transforming powers of love, even in this lament, are held up to the audience as the great generating force of human meaning in the *Meghadūta*.

Nor does the message itself end in despair. In 106 there is consolation in the form of stoical advice, and in 107 a vision of their union after the four remaining months of exile, at the end of Vishnu's sleep, which coincides with the rainy season. And in 108 the Yaksha adds a token of authenticity to the message by reminding his mate of an incident only the two could know.

fiers added to one element of a pair (as with "intense" in the fourth line). I have altered the grammar of the original in my version. Kālidāsa begins his series with paired nouns (with body body) and follows with five adjectival pairs modifying the nouns and matching them in inflection; I have shifted the modifying pairs to their noun forms because the adjective construction seemed to me strained in English. For a more faithfully literal rendering of this extraordinary passage, see Edgerton, *op. cit.*, p. 73, stanza 98.

With superb tact he chooses a humorous one that might help in cheering her up. Finally, he concludes (109) on a solemn note with two generalizations that, taken together, are calculated to assure her of his unshakable fidelity: first, the false commonplace that gossips cite—that passion dies in the absence of the lover; and, last, the true one—that passions grow with absence. One function of generalizations, as noted earlier, is to justify what might seem hard to believe, and that is the point of this one, which is aimed at cancelling its unsettling opposite. This last assurance is thus underwritten, so to speak, by common wisdom.

Stanzas 110–111: The two final stanzas resemble the end of formal supplication: they cite the cloud's generosity to other petitioners who have received what they requested even though the cloud remained, as it is now, silent. The cloud then is offered two honorable motives for performing the Yaksha's errand and finally dismissed with a blessing that once more affirms loving relationship. For in praying that the cloud never be separated from its mate, the lightning, as the Yaksha has been from his, a profound natural affinity between all lovers is implied. Separation, then, must be regarded as unnatural and, as such, a cause of pain as intense as that felt at amputation.

Here the poem closes, the cloud having "joined" the lovers as well as all else in the scope of its world.

Appendix II
Finding List

Agni(43*) A deity, "Fire," who because of his role in fire-oblations is traditionally seen as messenger to the gods.

Airāvata (62) A great elephant, *Indra's* vehicle.

Alakā (7, 63) *Kubera's* capital city, on a Himālayan peak (Mount *Kailāsa*).

Āmrakūta (17) Literally, "Mango-peak." One of the *Vindhya* mountains.

Arjuna (48) Great hero, leader of the Pāṇḍavas in the epic, *Mahābhārata*.

ashoka (75) A moderate-sized tree with large red flowers, reputed to blossom when kicked by a beautiful woman.

Avantī (30) A region whose capital is *Ujjayinī*.

Balarāma (49, 59) Brother of *Krishna*, usually considered a partial avatar of *Vishnu*.

Bali (57) A demon cleverly thwarted by *Vishnu* who first approached Bali as a dwarf and then grew to enormous size.

Bhavānī (36), 44) (Same as *Gaurī*.) Name of *Shiva's* wife in her amiable form. (See *Chaṇḍī*.).

*Numbers in parentheses refer to the stanzas in which a term occurs or is referred to.

111

Bhrigu's lord (57) Parashurāma, "Rāma of the Axe," a brahman who is said to have slain the entire kshatriya caste.

Brahmāvarta (48) The region, northwest of Hastinapura, between the *Sarasvatī* and *Drishadvatī* rivers. Also, its people.

chakravākī (80) (Fem. of chakravāka.) A bird, reputed to be separated each night from its mate, for whom it constantly cries.

Chandī (33) Name of *Shiva's* wife in her terrifying form. (See *Bhavānī*, *Gaurī*.)

chātaka (9, 21, 110) A bird, said to subsist on raindrops.

collyrium (92) A dark, glossy eye unguent, used here in the sense of mascara.

conch and lotus (77) Two of *Kubera's* so-called "nine treasures," considered to be auspicious signs.

Dashapura (47) *Rantideva's* capital city, the name of which means "ten-cities."

Dashārṇa (23) Name of a people, or their region.

Devagiri (42) A mountain. Literally, "Mountain of the Gods."

elephant guards of the Eight Directions (14) Massive elephants said to support the sky at the eight compass points.

field of the Kurus (Kurukshetra) (48) A battlefield, named after one of the contending families in the *Mahābhārata*.

Gambhīrā (40) A river, the name of which means "Possessed of Depth."

Gandhavatī (33) A river, the name of which means "Fragrant."

Gangā (43, 50, 63) The river Ganges, in North India, often personified as the second wife of *Shiva* and rival of *Gaurī*.

Gaurī (50, 60) (Same as *Bhavānī*.) *Shiva's* wife in her amiable form. (See *Chandī*.)

God of Love (71) Kāma or "Love" incarnate, counterpart of the Western Cupid. According to legend, burnt to ashes by the angry *Shiva* whom he foolishly tried to shoot with his love-arrows.

Hanumān (97) Name of a monkey or monkey-god and *Rāma's* faithful lieutenant, who located *Rāma's* wife, *Sītā*, after her abduction by the demon *Rāvaṇa*.

Hara (44) (Same as *Shiva.*)

Indra (6, 43) Chief of the gods, or devas, but subservient to the great gods (*Shiva, Vishnu*).

Jahnu (50) An irascible holy man who temporarily swallowed the *Gangā* on its way to earth. (See *Sagara.*)

Jahnu's daughter (50) (Same as *Gangā.*)

kadamba (25) A tree whose fragrant orange-colored blossoms are often used as hair ornaments.

Kailāsa (11, 58) A great Himālayan peak, said to be the abode of *Shiva* as well as the site of *Kubera's* city, *Alakā.*

kakubha (22) A tree, or its large fragrant flowers.

Kanakhala (50) A sacred mountain.

kandalī (21, 74, 93) The plantain tree. Often, its smooth trunk is compared to a woman's thighs.

kesara (21) The stamen of a flower, particularly the lotus. (75) A tree with white flowers, said to blossom when a beautiful woman sprays it with a mouthful of wine.

ketaka (23) A tree with beautiful flowers.

Kinnaras (56) Here, semi-divine beings, celestial singers and musicians.

Krauncha (57) A mountain in the eastern Himālayas, said to have been split in two by *Skanda.*

Krishna (15, 46) An incarnation of *Vishnu*, here appearing in his youthful role as a cowherd noted for his charm and great beauty.

Kubera (3, 7, 72) Originally, lord of demons. But in Kālidāsa's time god of riches, regent of the North, and chief of the *Yakshas.*

kutaja (4) A tree, the name of which means "Born in a Pitcher."

lac (32) A red dye used to ornament women's nails, hands, and feet.

lodhra (65) A tree with yellow flowers. Red powder made from its bark is scattered during the Holī festival. But the reference here must be to its light-colored pollen.

Lord of Beasts (56) (Same as *Shiva.*)

Lord of Heights (62) (Same as Mount *Kailāsa.*)

Lord of the Peaks (50) Himālaya.

Lord of the Raghus (12) (Same as *Rāma.*)

mādhavī (75) A creeper blooming in the spring.

Mahākāla (34) A place sacred to *Shiva* when he assumes the form of the destroyer of the world.

mālatī (95) A plant with fragrant white flowers which open in the evening.

Mānasa (11, 62, 73) A holy Himālayan lake on Mount *Kailāsa*, said to be the yearly retreat of wild geese.

mandāra (72) coral tree.

moonstone (67) A gem said to be made of congealed moonlight, and which supposedly melts under the influence of the moon's rays.

Nichais (25) The name of a mountain, literally meaning "low," "short," "small."

nichula (14, 41) Rattan cane, reeds.

nūpa (21, 65) (Same as *kadamba.*)

Nirvindhyā (28) As its name indicates, a river flowing from the *Vindhya* mountains.

Rāma (As in *Rāmagiri.*) The exiled hero of a great Indian epic, husband of *Sītā*, slayer of the demon, *Rāvaṇa.* Said to be an avatar of *Vishnu.*

Rāmagiri (1, 98) "*Rāma's* Mountain," in central India, where *Rāma* spent the beginning of his exile.

Rantideva (45) A king who spent his riches in pious sacrifices. The blood of the sacrificed animals was changed into a river, the Charmaṇvatī.

Rāvaṇa (58) A great demon king in the *Rāmayaṇa* epic, slain by *Rāma.*

Revā (19) A sacred river flowing westward from Mount *Āmrakūṭa* in the *Vindhya* mountains.

Revatī (49) Wife of *Balarāma.*

Sagara (50) A king whose sixty thousand sons—reduced to ashes by an angry sage—were given their funeral oblation when their descendent, Bhagīratha, led the *Gangā* River down from heaven.

Sarasvatī (49) A name sometimes identified with an ancient *Brahmāvarta* river.

sarikā (82) The myna bird.

shaphara (40) A small, bright-colored fish. Perhaps a minnow.

sharabha (54) A mythical, eight-legged deer, said to be extremely strong. An inhabitant of snowy regions.

Shiprā (31) A river, on whose banks is *Ujjayinī*.

shirīsha (65) A tree, or its flowers.

Shiva (7, 33, 36, 43, 50, 55, 58, 60, 71) The great divinity, usually represented as an ascetic and rivalled only by *Vishnu*.

shyāma (101) The word means "black" or "dark." Here, it refers to a thin kind of creeper.

Siddhas (14, 45, 55) Semi-divine beings of great purity and perfection, said to possess magic faculties.

Sindhu (29) Here, probably a river in Mālvā. (46) A river in general. (Here, the *Charmanvatī*, described in stanza 45.)

Sītā (1, 97) Devoted wife of *Rāma*, who voluntarily shared his exile on *Rāmagiri* until she was abducted by the demon *Rāvana*.

Skanda (43, 44) The god of war, son of *Shiva* and *Gaurī*.

The Triple-eyed God (52) (Same as *Shiva*.)

Tripura (56) Three demon cities destroyed by *Shiva*.

Udayana (30) Fabled king of Vatsa whose romance with Vāsavadattā, treated many times in story and drama, was popular among the people of *Ujjayinī*.

Ujjayinī (27) (Same as *Vishālā*.) The capital city of *Avantī*—one of seven cities sacred to the Hindus.

Vetravatī (24) A river flowing from the *Vindhya* mountains to its confluence with the *Yamunā* River.

Vidishā (24) The capital city of the *Dashārna* country.

Vindhya (19) Name of a vast mountain range stretching across the middle of India.

Vishālā (30) (Same as *Ujjayinī*.)

Vishnu (15, 57, 107) The great god, rivalled only by *Shiva*, who periodically appears on earth to destroy evil. His most famous incarnations are *Rāma* and *Krishna*.

white bull (of *Shiva*) (52) *Shiva's* vehicle, called Nandī.

Wishing Tree (62, 66) A tree said to have the power to grant all desires.

Yaksha (1, 5, 7, 66, 69) A class of semi-divine beings, usually benign, ruled over by *Kubera*.

Yamunā (51) A great North Indian river, flowing from a Himālayan peak to its confluence with the *Gangā* River.

ceremonial quality

political advice 6

oppression 53
need for goals 54
purgation 55
Alaka 63-64